はじめに

　本書は，開隆堂版高校英語教科書 APPLAUSE ENGLISH COMMUNICATION I に完全準拠したワークブックです。各 Lesson の Section ごとの内容把握と単語や重要表現，まとめの問題のほか，総合問題などを収録しています。教科書と同様に音声を QR コードから確認することができます。

Contents

JN045735

1 【本文理解】音声を聞いて，区切りに気をつけて音読し，下の問いに答えましょう。

There are many places / with beautiful scenery / in the world. // G We sometimes see
 V   S   S   V

these pictures. // G They are really impressive. //
 O   S   V   C

G Look at this picture. // This is an aurora / with various colors. // ❶It is amazing. // It
 (S)V   S   V   C   S V   C

is a natural light display, / and it is like a beautiful light show / in the sky. //

These are heart-shaped islands. // ❷They are romantic. // They are not artificial
 S   V   C   S   V   C   S   V   C

islands. //

When people see these pictures, / they probably want to visit / these places. // Would

you like to visit / these places? //
 S   V   O

(1) 下線部❶ It は何を指すのか，文中の５語で答えましょう。

( )

(2) 下線部❷ They は何を指すのか，文中の２語で答えましょう。

( )

2 【単語】次の語句の意味を調べて書きましょう。

(1) amazing* 形( )   (2) scenery 名( )

(3) impressive 形( )   (4) aurora 名( )

(5) various* 形( )   (6) display* 名( )

(7) romantic 形( )   (8) artificial 形( )

(9) probably* 副( )

Nice Fit 本文から抜き出しましょう。 ハート型の島＝( ) ( )

Coffee Break

beautiful（お尻につけて名詞から形容詞）
beautiful の -ful のように，お尻につけて名詞から形容詞になるものに，下記のようなものがあります。
-al, -ous, -ic, -y, -able, -ive, -ible, -ish, -ly

英会話
footwork Where do you like to go on weekends?

APPLAUSE
ENGLISH COMMUNICATION I

WORKBOOK
解答・解説

1 (1) an aurora with various colors
  (2) heart-shaped islands
2 (1) すばらしい, 驚くべき
  (2) 景色
  (3) 印象的な
  (4) オーロラ
  (5) さまざまな
  (6) 演技, 見世物
  (7) ロマンチックな, すてきな
  (8) 人工的な
  (9) たぶん

Nice Fit

heart-shaped islands

3 (1) My grandmother lives in the country
  (2) That building is very high
  (3) I like her songs
  (4) My sister looked pretty in her pink dress
4 (1) like
  (2) would, to
5 ウ

解説

2 (4) aurora—The Top 10 Most Beautiful English Words(2021) の第6位です。
3 (1) S V（第1文型）
  (2) S V C（第2文型） S＝C
  (3) S V O（第3文型） S≠O
  (4) S V C（第2文型） S＝C
    前置詞句(in〜)や副詞(very)は文型の要素とはみなさない。
4 (1) 接続詞の like(〜のように)と動詞の like(〜が好きである)を区別しよう。
  (2) would like to do：好み・支払方法・余暇の過ごし方など意向を述べる言い方です。
5 質問文の when they see these beautiful pictures に着目すると, ウの They want to visit these places が導き出される。

1 (1) the ruins
  (2) 人間に環境が変えられてきていること。
2 (1) 遺産
  (2) 遺跡
  (3) 桜の花
  (4) 反射, （水に映った)影
  (5) 廃墟, 遺跡
  (6) 城
  (7) 県
  (8) 絵画
  (9) 平和
  (10) 心, 精神
  (11) 気にする
  (12) 環境

Nice Fit

its reflection in the lake

3 (1) I gave my sister a doll
  (2) gave Freddie a CD yesterday
  (3) my father bought me a new dictionary
  (4) showed us the way to the station
4 (1) looks like
  (2) care about
5 (1) T
  (2) F
  (3) T
  (4) F

解説

3 基本的に「人に・物を」の語順で第4文型（S V O O）は完成します。
4 (1) look like：まるで〜のように見える
  (2) don't care about：〜を気にしない
5 (1) 本文1行目で言及されている。
  (2) 富士山はすでに世界遺産に登録されている。
  (3) 本文4〜5行目にそう記述されている。
  (4) 本文の最後に逆の内容が書かれている。

『APPLAUSE ENGLISH COMMUNICATION I Workbook』

解答　正誤表

上記書籍に誤りがありました。心よりお詫び申し上げますとともに、下記の通りご訂正くださいますようお願いいたします。

箇所	誤	正
p.18 左段 5 (6)	ⓒ F	ⓒ T
p.18 左段 解説 5 (6)	ⓒの解説文	削除
p.21 右段 1 (1)	ice hokey	ice hockey

開隆堂出版

1 (1) カラスの
  (2) the change of the seasons
2 (1) 枕
  (2) 夜明け
  (3) (朝・1日が)始まる
  (4) 徐々に
  (5) ホタル
  (6) 飛び回る
  (7) 日没
  (8) カラス
  (9) 巣
  (10) 役に立つ
  (11) 消える
  (12) 気候

Nice Fit

the change of the seasons

3 (1) They named their child Rome
  (2) The news made her happy
  (3) They named their first child George
  (4) The news made him sad
4 (1) four seasons
  (2) going back
5 エ

解説

3 第5文型(SVOC)では，O＝Cの関係が成り立ちます。
  (1) their child＝Rome
  (2) her＝happy
  (3) their first child＝George
  (4) him＝sad
4 (1) 四季：the four seasons
  (2) 帰る：go back(現在進行形にすると未来の意味を表現することができる)
5 本文5～6行目に「冬はつとめて。雪の降りたるは，言ふべきにもあらず」に相当する描写が見られる。

1 (1) artificial
  (2) lake
  (3) pillow
  (4) aurora
  (5) memorize [remember]
2 (解答例) Japan has four seasons and beautiful nature. Sei-Shonagon wrote about them. But the climate is changing now.
3 (1) Why do you look so happy
  (2) She showed me the way to
  (3) The man made her happy
  (4) There is a map on the desk
4 (1) turned pale
  (2) runs, at
  (3) let, alone
5 (1) with
  (2) Would you like to visit these places
  (3) ③ World Heritage
    ⑤ four seasons
  (4) 富士山とその湖に写る影は，桜の花と共に美しく見えます。
  (5) ア 四季の変化 イ (とても)有益
  (6) people, care about, environment

解説

3 (3) make＋O＋C OをCにする
4 (2) run(自動詞) 経営・運営・管理する
5 (1) with 句は前の名詞を修飾する。
  (2) Would you like to do? …したいですか，…することをどう思いますか？
  (5) find 偶然・経験・試みによってO〈人・物・事〉が…とわかる
  (6) 美しい景色が損なわれている原因を答える。問題文第2段落後半に some people don't care about the environment とある。

1 (1) chocolate
　(2) cacao beans
2 (1) 神秘的な
　(2) 固体の
　(3) アステカ族の
　(4) 帝国
　(5) 皇帝
　(6) モンテスマ
　(7) カカオ
　(8) 豆
　(9) さや，（カカオの）実
　(10) 含む
　(11) 通貨
　(12) 穀物

Nice Fit

used them as a currency

3 (1) taught us that
　(2) knows that
　(3) hear that
　(4) says that
4 (1) is made from
　(2) In those days
5 (1) T
　(2) F
　(3) T
　(4) F

解説
3 that 節を「ひとかたまり」としてとらえる
　ことが大切となる。したがって，音読する場
　合は that の直前で区切る。
4 (1) 見ただけでは何からできているのかわか
　　らない場合は from を用いるのが原則。
5 (1) 本文2行目で言及されている。
　(2) 15杯ではなく，50杯飲んだ。
　(3) 本文5行目にその記述が見られる。
　(4) food for thought「思考の糧，考える材
　　料」についての記述はない。

1 (1) the Spanish
　(2) the great invention [a British company]
2 (1) スペイン人
　(2) 征服する
　(3) 最初は
　(4) 嫌う
　(5) 高貴な，貴族の
　(6) （気分などを）新鮮にする
　(7) 発明
　(8) ココア
　(9) バター
　(10) ～の代わりに
　(11) ～を超えて
　(12) 歴史的に

Nice Fit

a solid food

3 (1) heavier
　(2) larger
　(3) more popular
　(4) more useful
4 (1) instead of
　(2) all over the world
5 エ

解説
3 (1) 活用：heavy－heavier－the heaviest
　(2) 活用：large — larger－the largest
　(3) 活用：popular－more popular－the most popular
　(4) 活用：useful－more useful－the most useful
4 (1) …しないで：instead of ～
　(2) 世界中に：all over the world, throughout the world
5 液状チョコレートを固体に変容させた経緯
　を答える。本文5～6行目に，イギリスの会
　社がお湯の代わりに粉末ココアを使用したと
　の記述がある。

Lesson 2 — The Mysterious History of Chocolate ❸ pp.14-15

1 (1) a chocolate beverage
　(2) cacao polyphenol

2 (1) オランダ人
　(2) 飲み物
　(3) まれな，珍しい
　(4) 海外へ
　(5) 広がる
　(6) ～の至るところに
　(7) ～に加えて
　(8) 科学的な
　(9) ポリフェノール
　(10) 健康
　(11) ～を下げる
　(12) 図表，グラフ

Nice Fit

lower blood pressure

3 (1) as fast as
　(2) the shortest of
　(3) the most famous
　(4) the most important

4 (1) In addition to
　(2) for example

5 (1) F
　(2) F
　(3) F
　(4) F

解説

3 (1) as ～ as ...　同等比較表現
　(2) 最上級：short → the shortest(of all)
　(3) 最上級：famous → the most famous
　(4) 最上級：important → the most important

4 副詞用法の慣用句は繰り返して覚えよう。

5 (1) 史実によれば板チョコではなかった。
　(2) gradually(徐々に)との記述がある。
　(3) 砂糖ではなく，ポリフェノールが効く。
　(4) 「リンゴの4倍」と記述されている。

Lesson 2 — The Mysterious History of Chocolate まとめ pp.16-17

1 (1) currency
　(2) sugar
　(3) gradually
　(4) chocolate
　(5) like [love]

2 (解答例)　The Dutch brought a chocolate beverage to Japan in the 18th century. It is one of the most popular sweets. In addition to that, chocolate is getting popular as healthy food.

3 (1) is the largest city in Japan
　(2) plays the piano better than
　(3) that he has lost his passport
　(4) is as valuable as time

4 (1) not as old as
　(2) know that, wants to
　(3) more beautiful than

5 (1) その当時，カカオ豆はとても貴重だったので，人々は通貨として使用した。
　(2) ② At first　　⑤ For example
　(3) ③ more　　④ most
　(4) ア 4倍　　イ ポリフェノール
　(5) ⓐ T　　ⓑ F　　ⓒ F

解説

3 (3) that 節が補語になっているケース。
　(4) Nothing is as ～ as ... で，…ほど～なものはない，つまり，…が最も～となり，最上級に相当する意味になる。

4 (1) not as A as B：BであるほどAでない

5 (1) 文中の they がカカオ豆を指していることを確認し，so ～ that ... に注意して訳す。
　(5) ⓐ 本文冒頭部分に同内容の記述がある。
　　ⓑ スペインではなく，イギリスの会社。
　　ⓒ 健康に良いのは，カフェインではなく，カカオ・ポリフェノールとされている。

1 (1) many students
(2) 1人の学生が複数の競技に参加すること。
2 (1) 部活動　(2) ふつう
(3) もちろん　(4) 考え
(5) 長所　(6) しかしながら
(7) 体系　(8) 練習する
(9) たとえば　(10) よく知られている
(11) 参加　(12) 複数の

Nice Fit

have a season system

3 (1) I have been to Canada twice
(2) has gone to Bali on vacation
(3) has been absent from school
(4) have known him for five years
4 (1) is familiar to
(2) What do you think of
5 (1) T
(2) T
(3) T
(4) F

解説

3 (1) have been to 「経験」用法
(2) has gone to 「結果」用法
(3) has been absent 「継続」用法
(4) have known him 「継続」用法
4 (1) 定形表現：be familiar to 〜
(2) 定形表現：What do you think of 〜?
＝How do you feel about 〜?
5 (1) 本文1行目に同内容の記述がある。
(2) 本文1〜2行目でそう言及されている。
(3) 本文3〜4行目で同趣旨の内容が述べられている。
(4) 部活動にシーズン・システムを導入しているのは, 日本ではなくアメリカ合衆国である。

1 (1) students
(2) some students in Japan
2 (1) 利点　(2) 獲得する
(3) 経験　(4) 向上させる
(5) 筋肉　(6) 忍耐
(7) 可能にする　(8) 可能性
(9) 反復的な, 繰り返しの
(10) 緊張させる, 痛める
(11) 作用する, 影響を及ぼす
(12) 発達

Nice Fit

the development of muscles

3 (1) have been sleeping for
(2) has been talking on
(3) has been raining since
(4) has been flying since
4 (1) enabled, to
(2) since an early age
5 エ

解説

First, や Second, For example, In this case, などの談話標識（Discourse Markers）に着目すると, 内容理解の効率が飛躍的に伸びます。

3 (1) have been sleeping ずっと寝ている
(2) has been talking 話し続けている
(3) has been raining ずっと降っている
(4) has been flying 飛び続けている
現在完了進行形では, for と since の使い分けが重要となる。⇒「期間」を表すときは for,「起点」を表す場合は since を用いる。
4 (1) 無生物主語＋enable (s, d) ＋人＋to do 「人が…することを可能にする」
(2) since an early age 「幼少より」
5 'the possibility of injury'という文言の近くにある because が導く節が正解となる。

1 (1) swimming and rugby
　(2) Shibuno Hinako
2 (1) ～が得意である
　(2) 水泳選手
　(3) やめる
　(4) ～が原因で
　(5) 人気のある
　(6) プロの
　(7) ゴルファー
　(8) ゴルフ
　(9) ～のおかげで
　(10) 訓練する，鍛える
　(11) 向上させる
　(12) トーナメント

Nice Fit

a popular professional golfer
3 (1) he had borrowed from her
　(2) had lived here before I
　(3) had never seen
　(4) had already stopped
4 (1) not only, but also
　(2) experiences in playing
5 (1) T
　(2) F
　(3) F
　(4) F

解説
3 過去完了の文は，基準となる過去のある時点を示す表現と共に用いられることが多い。
　(1) 基準：He lost the umbrella …
　(2) 基準：… before I moved to Zushi.
　(3) 基準：… till she died.
　(4) 基準：… when I got home.
5 (1) 最終段落に該当する記述が見られる。
　(2) スキーヤーではなく水泳選手だった。
　(3) ソフトテニスではなくソフトボール。
　(4) 本文の最後の文に「可能だ」とある。

1 (1) familiar [popular]
　(2) basketball
　(3) athlete
　(4) increase
　(5) endure, bear, tolerate, stand
2 (解答例) Multiple sports have many advantages for young people.　First, they acquire various abilities.　Second, they can build their bodies and decrease the chance of injury.
3 (1) I have lost
　(2) had lived in
　(3) I had bought
　(4) has been crying
4 (1) have never been to Taiwan
　(2) had been sick in bed
　(3) has been playing the violin
　(4) How long have you been in Paris
5 (1) multiple sports experiences enable young students to build their bodies
　(2) ② In this case 　⑤ Thanks to
　(3) are good at, too
　(4) オ
　(5) さまざまなことをするときにトップアスリートだけでなく私たちの誰もが自分自身を向上させることができる
　(6) repetitive movements, development of muscles

解説
3 (1)および(4) (1)は「未だ見つかっていない」，(4)は「今も泣いている」という内容より，現在完了形がふさわしい。
　(6) 質問文内にある possibility, injury, increase 等のキーワードに着目して本文を読み進めると，該当する because 節を見つけることができる。

1 (1)　Wright Flyer
　(2)　約36.5メートルを12秒間飛んだこと。
2 (1)　進化する
　(2)　飛行機
　(3)　古代の
　(4)　ついに
　(5)　有人の
　(6)　ライトフライヤー号
　(7)　ガソリン
　(8)　プロペラ
　(9)　まったく初めての
　(10)　飛行
　(11)　人間

Nice Fit

the very first flight in history

3 (1)　can
　(2)　must
　(3)　May
　(4)　may
4 (1)　small step, giant
　(2)　in various ways
5 (1)　F
　(2)　F
　(3)　T
　(4)　F
　(5)　T

解説

3 (1)　「～できます」 can do
　(2)　「～せねばなりません」 must do
　(3)　「～してよろしいですか」 May I do ～?
　(4)　「～かもしれない」 may be
5 (1)　スカイダイビングについては記述なし。
　(2)　二人は実の兄弟である。
　(3)　およそ120年前のことである。
　(4)　3～4行目にライトフライヤーとある。
　(5)　最後の文にその記述が見られる。

1 (1)　this (new) type of airplane
　(2)　New types of engines
2 (1)　会社
　(2)　発明する
　(3)　天井
　(4)　屋外用の
　(5)　乗客
　(6)　バイオ燃料
　(7)　電気
　(8)　太陽光の
　(9)　環境にやさしい
　(10)　騒音
　(11)　マッハ
　(12)　～につき

Nice Fit

in the future

3 (1)　is liked by
　(2)　wasn't invited
　(3)　Was she scolded
　(4)　was found
4 (1)　What, like
　(2)　day by day
　(3)　Are, able to
5　ア

解説

3　〈by ～〉が「重要な情報」である場合のみ
〈by ～〉で動作主(＝行為者)を表す。(2), (4)
の場合は不要。
　(2)　動作主が不要・自明の場合
　(4)　動作主が不明の場合
4 (1)　What is S like? 〈人・物・事は〉「ど
のようなものか」？ 「どういう様子か」？
おおよその概念・性格・外観などを尋ね
る。
5　本文中の'so it is lighter'という箇所に着
目することができれば,「材質の軽量化」とい
う答えが得られる。

1 (1)　flight attendants
　(2)　meal services
　(3)　the airplane seats

2 (1)　接客係，添乗員　　(2)　機能的な
　(3)　伝統的な　　(4)　保証する
　(5)　快適さ
　(6)　呼び物，目玉商品
　(7)　航空会社　　(8)　種類
　(9)　軽食　　(10)　宗教
　(11)　選択肢
　(12)　～に基づいて
　(13)　工学　　(14)　絶えず，いつも

Nice Fit

　　board an airplane

3 (1)　can be seen
　(2)　should be kept
　(3)　must, be forgotten [forgot]
　(4)　will be held

4 (1)　with a smile
　(2)　What kind of
　(3)　on the basis

5 (1)　F
　(2)　F
　(3)　F
　(4)　T

解説

3　助動詞を含む受動態の肯定文は，〈助動詞＋be＋過去分詞〉となる。否定文は，〈助動詞＋not＋be＋過去分詞〉となる。
　(1)　「見られる」 can be seen
　(2)　「守るべき」 should be kept
　(3)　「忘れてはならぬ」 must not be forgotten
　(4)　「開かれるだろう」will be held

5 (1)　本文3行目に are also <u>changing</u> とある。
　(2)　本文4行目に is often <u>the meal</u> とある。
　(3)　本文7行目に <u>other food options</u> are available とある。
　(4)　<u>evolving</u> = developing and changing

---

1 (1)　fly
　(2)　eco-friendly
　(3)　uniform
　(4)　ceiling
　(5)　soon

2 （解答例） The Wright brothers were able to fly an airplane in 1903. This was the very first flight in history. Now, an airplane can carry more than five hundred people.

3 (1)　By whom was this table made?
　(2)　I will be invited to the prom by Mary.
　(3)　She was seen to sing at the stage by Saburo.
　(4)　No attention was paid to her words by them.

4 (1)　He can speak English fluently
　(2)　can't have read this book
　(3)　must be sent at once
　(4)　will be put off till next week

5 (1)　① could　② can　③ won't
　(2)　エ
　(3)　将来，飛行機はどのようなものになるのでしょうか。
　(4)　The speed is expected to be Mach 4.5
　(5)　ⓐ　were able to
　　　ⓑ　fewer materials

解説

3 (1)　動作主を尋ねる受動態の疑問文：Who was this table made by? も可。
　(2)　助動詞 will を含む受動態
　(3)　〈S＋知覚動詞V＋O＋原形不定詞〉の受動態：原形不定詞は to- 不定詞になる。
　(4)　pay attention to を句動詞としてひとまとめに扱って，Her words were paid no attention to by them. とすることもできる。

5 (2)　名詞の強調〈the ／ this ／ that ／所有格の人称代名詞＋very＋名詞〉「まさに～，～こそ」

9

Lesson 5 — The Symbol of Peace ❶ pp.34-35

1 (1) Sapeurs
 (2) very expensive fashionable clothes
2 (1) 流行の，はやりの
 (2) 郊外
 (3) 共和国
 (4) 進歩，向上
 (5) 上品な
 (6) 貧しい
 (7) 収入
 (8) 裕福な
 (9) そしてまた～ない
 (10) 流行
 (11) 平日
 (12) ふだんの，堅苦しくない
 (13) 毎月の
 (14) 給料

Nice Fit

in a suburb

3 (1) Eating too much
 (2) taking pictures of
 (3) talking with
 (4) reading, novels
4 (1) Nor do I
 (2) much more carefully
5 (1) T
 (2) F
 (3) F
 (4) T

解説
3 (1) 主語として使われた動名詞
 (2) 補語として使われた動名詞
 (3) enjoy の後ろは動名詞が来る。
 (4) 前置詞の目的語としての動名詞
4 (1) Neither do I. も可。
5 (1) 本文冒頭部分が該当する。
 (2) richest ではなく poorest が正しい。
 (3) 6行目に，平日は「普通の人」とある。
 (4) 7～8行目に同内容の記述がある。

Lesson 5 — The Symbol of Peace ❷ pp.36-37

1 (1) Republic of Congo
 (2) Sapeurs
2 (1) 植民地化する
 (2) 独立
 (3) 国内の，市民の
 (4) 起こる
 (5) 暴力
 (6) モットー
 (7) 武器
 (8) 優雅に
 (9) デザイナーによって作られた
 (10) 虚栄心
 (11) ふるまう
 (12) 称賛する

Nice Fit

several civil wars

3 (1) To master English is not easy
 (2) bought some books to read
 (3) My job was to wash
 (4) a man to help us
4 (1) Let us
 (2) as a symbol of
5 イ

解説
3 (1) 主語としての名詞的用法の不定詞
 (2) 形容詞的用法の不定詞(～するため用の)
 (3) 補語としての名詞的用法の不定詞
 (4) 形容詞的用法の不定詞(～をしてくれるための)
4 (1) Let's は Let us が短縮されたもの。公式な演説の中などで多用される傾向がある。
 (2) 類例：The dove is loved as a symbol of peace.
5 they do not fight の前に'so'があり，その直前が理由を表していると考えられる。

10

1 (1) Republic of Congo
　(2) Democratic Republic of the Congo
2 (1) 共和国
　(2) 民主主義の
　(3) 〜である一方
　(4) 前者の
　(5) 正式の
　(6) スーツ
　(7) 後者の
　(8) 服装一式
　(9) 〜だけれども
　(10) 議長
　(11) 協会
　(12) 予防接種

Nice Fit

a vaccination for peace

3 (1) エ
　(2) ア
　(3) ウ
　(4) オ
　(5) イ
4 (1) One the, other
　(2) to look out for each
5 ① poor
　② wearing
　③ make
　④ symbol
　⑤ both
　⑥ wish
　⑦ chairman

解説

3 (1) 感情・心情の原因を表すエが来る。
　(2) 成長・発展の結果を表すアが正解。
　(3) 目的を表すウが正答。
　(4) 形式主語に対する真主語のオが適切。
　(5) 判断の根拠を・基準を表すイが続く。

1 (1) weekend
　(2) dirty
　(3) outfit [garment]
　(4) suburb
　(5) represent [embody]
2 （解答例）Republic of Congo was colonized by France from 1882 to 1960. After its independence, people wanted to spend a peaceful life. They thought that one way to make the country peaceful was by dressing up.
3 (1) She decided to climb Mt. Fuji alone
　(2) something cold to drink
　(3) grew up to be a teacher
　(4) It is easy for him to solve
4 (1) playing the guitar
　(2) finished reading
　(3) be afraid of making
　(4) enjoyed watching, on TV
5 (1) a. suburb　b. casual　c. motto
　(2) ① called　　② countries
　　　④ wearing　⑤ to spend
　　　⑦ dressing
　(3) either
　(4) イ
　(5) 私たちは軍隊の靴ではなく，デザイナーブランドの靴をはいて音を立てるべきです。
　(6) ⓐ F　　ⓑ F　　ⓒ T

解説

4 (1) stop -ing （〜をやめる）
　(2) finish -ing （〜を終わらせる）
　(3) 前置詞の目的語に適する形は -ing 形
　(4) enjoy -ing （〜して楽しむ）
cf. 迷ったときは p.34 Coffee Break 欄にある **Daic Megafeps** を思い出そう。
5 (4) 形容詞的用法の不定詞を含む文はイ。
　(6) ⓐ Brasilia ではなく，Brazzaville。
　　　ⓑ 彼らは決して裕福なわけではない。
　　　ⓒ 第3段落に同内容の記述がある。

1 (1) George Crum　(2) the potatoes
2 (1) 運よく見つけたもの
　(2) 価値のある
　(3) がみがみと口うるさい
　(4) 金持ち，富豪
　(5) シェフ，料理長
　(6) 料理をする
　(7) 極度に，極端に
　(8) 丸まる
　(9) パリパリした
　(10) 突き刺す
　(11) フォーク
　(12) 薄切り，小片
　(13) 起こる，生じる
　(14) 怒り

Nice Fit

got really angry

3 (1) at this sleeping baby
　(2) fish swimming in the pond
　(3) the excited audience
　(4) some photos taken during the tour
4 (1) by accident　(2) originate from
5 (1) F
　(2) T
　(3) F
　(4) T

解説

2 (1) serendipity—The Top 10 Most Beautiful English Words (2021) の第10位です。
3 (1) sleeping baby 1 語なので前置修飾
　(2) fish swimming in the pond 後置修飾
　(3) excited audience 1 語なので前置修飾
　(4) photos taken during the tour 後置修飾
5 (1) as expected ではなく by accident (偶然)。
　(2) 関連した逸話が5行目に見られる。
　(3) 客を追い出すことはしていない。
　(4) 文章全体の要旨に合致している。

1 (1) this strange glue
　(2) Art (Fry)
2 (1) 化学者
　(2) 接着剤，のり
　(3) くっつく
　(4) 容易に
　(5) 失敗
　(6) 顕微鏡
　(7) 同僚
　(8) はがす
　(9) だれが～を望むのか (だれも～を望まない)
　(10) しおり
　(11) うわあ
　(12) 接着剤のついた，接着性の

Nice Fit

sticky notes were first created
3 (1) heard the boy call my name
　(2) see the man enter the room
　(3) heard something move in
　(4) I felt my interest rising
4 (1) happen to know
　(2) said to themselves
5 エ

解説

3 (1) 知覚動詞 heard + O + call
　(2) 知覚動詞 see + O + enter
　(3) 知覚動詞 heard + O + move
　(4) 知覚動詞 felt + O + rising
4 (1) Do you know ～よりていねいな言い方
　(2) say to oneself「～と心の中で考える」
5 「付箋が誕生したのはいつのこと？」
　ア　1969年から5年後 (×)
　イ　この点については言及なし (×)
　ウ　Art であって Spencer ではない (×)
　エ　人物名，年代ともに適切 (○)

1 (1) the other seller [Ernest Hamwi]
 (2) the ice-cream seller

2 (1) 購入
 (2) 展示，会，博覧会
 (3) ミズーリ州
 (4) 売り手，売る人
 (5) アイスクリームの
 (6) 〜を使い果たす
 (7) ザラビア
 (8) ワッフル
 (9) ペーストリー
 (10) おい，よう
 (11) 兄弟
 (12) 代用品
 (13) 円錐状のもの，アイスクリームを入れる
   円錐形のウエハース
 (14) 現在の

the current ice-cream cone

3 (1) makes me go shopping
 (2) made one student sing the song
 (3) had the secretary send the mail
 (4) let me introduce myself

4 (1) are running out of
 (2) by mistake

5 (1) F
 (2) T
 (3) T
 (4) F

解説

3 (1) 使役動詞 makes + O + 原形 go
 (2) 使役動詞 made + O + 原形 sing
 (3) 使役動詞 had + O + 原形 send
 (4) 使役動詞 let + O + 原形 introduce

5 (1) 1904年に開催されたルイジアナ博覧会。
 (2) 1〜2行目に該当の記述がある。
 (3) 3行目で売り子がそう叫んでいる。
 (4) ザラビアを巻いたのは Hamwi である。

1 (1) serendipity
 (2) bookmark [bookmarker]
 (3) substitute (4) chef
 (5) encounter

2 (解答例) In 1853, a rich guest ordered French fries, and when he saw them, he sent them back again and again to the restaurant kitchen. The chef got really angry, and he cut the potatoes extremely thin like pieces of paper. Strangely enough, they became the first potato chips.

3 (1) of that sleeping dog
 (2) at this broken chair
 (3) you know the man running over there
 (4) What is the language spoken in Brazil

4 (1) made me wash
 (2) saw her go
 (3) felt someone touching

5 (1) making valuable discoveries by accident
 (2) ② too ④ thin
   ⑤ with ⑥ in
 (3) ウ
 (4) 5年後，アートは彼の本からしおりが落ちるのを見たときに，1つのアイデアが思い浮かびました。
 (5) ウ (6) chef's anger

解説

4 (1) 「〜させた」   使役動詞 made
 (2) 「〜を見た 」   知覚動詞 saw
 (3) 「〜を感じた」   知覚動詞 felt
 (4) 「〜をさせてくれた」使役動詞 let

5 (5) ア：紙綴器(ホッチキス)，イ：食物保存用のビニール袋(ジップロック)，ウ：付箋紙(ポストイット)，エ：保護テープ(マスキングテープ)

1 (1) Johannes Vermeer
(2) Vermeer's [his] works
2 (1) 展示する
(2) したがって
(3) 美術館
(4) 謎, 神秘
(5) 離れて, 去って
(6) ～歳のときに
(7) ～にかかわらず
(8) 傑作
(9) 展覧会
(10) 少なくとも
(11) 魅了する
(12) 魅力的

Nice Fit

all over the world

3 (1) the girl who can speak
(2) which was made in
(3) the man who helped me
(4) that produces cacao beans
4 (1) passed away
(2) at least, so far
(3) fascinated with
5 (1) F
(2) T
(3) F
(4) T

解説

3 (1) 先行詞：その女の子　← who 節
(2) 先行詞：オープンカー　← which 節
(3) 先行詞：その男性　← who 節
(4) 先行詞：唯一の州　← that 節
先行詞が最上級形容詞や序数詞, the only などを伴う場合は that を用いることが多い。
5 (1) 生誕年は正しいが, 出生地が異なる。
(2) 本文 2 ～ 3 行目に明示されている。
(3) poor works(駄作)どころか傑作である。
(4) 本文 5 行目に at the age of 43とある。

1 (1) (the color called) "Vermeer blue"
(2) lapis lazuli
2 (1) 魔術師　(2) 牛乳を注ぐ女
(3) 影　(4) 衣類
(5) 習得する　(6) 知覚, 認知
(7) 形態, 形状　(8) 特徴, 特色
(9) 真珠　(10) 耳飾り
(11) トルコの　(12) ターバン
(13) ラピスラズリ, るり
(14) 鉱物　(15) 純粋な
(16) それにもかかわらず
(17) 豊富に, 多量に

Nice Fit

in those days

3 (1) the lady whom I want to introduce to you
(2) the putter that my father bought yesterday
(3) the cap which you lost last week
(4) all the money that I have now
4 (1) In this way
(2) is made from
5 ウ

解説

3 (1) 先行詞：女性　introduce の目的語
(2) 先行詞：パター　bought の目的語
(3) 先行詞：帽子　lost の目的語
(4) 先行詞：お金　have の目的語
4 (1) 「このように」：(in)this way
(2) 「～から精製されている」：be made from ～
5 「ターバン風かぶり物」の歴史的意味が問われている。本文 8 行目にある'It shows ～'というディスコース・マーカー(談話標識)に着目すると, 正解を比較的容易に導き出すことができる。

Lesson 7	The Secrets Hidden in ❸ Vermeer's Works pp.54-55

1 (1)　much
　(2)　"Girl with a Pearl Earring"

2 (1)　～と比べて　　(2)　名声
　(3)　必ずしも　　(4)　借金，負債
　(5)　パン屋　　(6)　～を手渡す
　(7)　実際は，実のところ
　(8)　安く　　(9)　ギルダー
　(10)　金では買えない
　(11)　熱狂，情熱　　(12)　苦悩

Nice Fit

see his masterpieces first-hand

3 (1)　the boy whose bike [bicycle] was stolen
　(2)　the man whose sister is
　(3)　The house whose roof you can
　(4)　whose top is covered with snow

4 (1)　in contrast with
　(2)　made a living
　(3)　Why, first-hand

5 ①　reputation　②　valuable
　③　Spanish　④　distress
　⑤　what

解説

1 (1)　下線部❶の debt は「借金のある状態」という不可算名詞なので，much が正解。
　(2)　下線部❷の it は「真珠の耳飾りの少女」（1665～66年頃）という名画を指している。

3 (1)　bicycle は先行詞 the boy の所有物
　(2)　sister は先行詞 the man の所有物
　(3)　roof は先行詞 the house の付属物
　(4)　top は先行詞 the mountain の付属物

4 (1)　in contrast with：「～と比べて」
　(2)　make a living：「生計を立てる」
　(3)　Why don't you ～?：「～したらどう」

5　大きな仕事を成し遂げるも生前はまったく評価されず，当人が死亡した後に業績の大きさが評価されたフェルメールの運命を，幾つかのキーワードをもとに要約してまとめる。

Lesson 7	The Secrets Hidden in Vermeer's Works まとめ pp.56-57

1 (1)　museum　　(2)　milkmaid
　(3)　priceless　　(4)　masterpiece
　(5)　poor

2 （解答例）Vermeer's nickname is "the magician of light." As a painter, he made good use of light. Another characteristic is the use of color. He used the color called "Vermeer blue."

3 (1)　who is talking with [to]
　(2)　whose mother is a doctor
　(3)　who [whom, that] she loves
　(4)　which [that] the boy gave

4 (1)　The woman who [whom, that] I met at the airport was a Chinese
　(2)　Look at the boy and his dog that are running after a fox
　(3)　I will show you the smartphone which [that] I bought the day before yesterday
　(4)　I'm so sorry to hear about the girl whose bike was stolen

5 (1)　ア
　(2)　② which　　⑥ whose
　(3)　③ those days　　④ contrast with
　　⑤ fact
　(4)　フェルメールには，既に完璧であるものをさらにより完璧にしようとする情熱と苦悩があった。
　(5)　ⓐ　left　　ⓑ　gold
　　ⓒ　bread　　ⓓ　death

解説

4　目的格の関係詞節の中に目的語を置き忘れ（書き残し）てしまうミスに注意する。
　(1)　[誤] The woman whom I met her at the airport was a Chinese.
　(3)　[誤] I will show you the smartphone which I bought it the day before yesterday.

15

Endangered Species ❶ in the World
pp.58-59

1 (1) 5,500 mammals
  (2) these animals
2 (1) 絶滅の危機にある
  (2) 100万(の)
  (3) 増加，成長
  (4) 連合
  (5) 保護，保全
  (6) リストアップする
  (7) 驚くべきことに
  (8) 哺乳類
  (9) 絶滅した
  (10) 極の
  (11) ゴリラ
  (12) サイ

Nice Fit

world population growth

3 (1) about which
  (2) of whom
  (3) in which
  (4) on which
4 (1) suffering from
  (2) out of
5 エ

解説

1 (1) 1,219頭は5,500頭の約22%になることから，下線部❶の them は5,500 mammals であることがわかる。

3 元の英文を想定して関係代名詞の前に移動させる「前置詞」を特定する。
  (1) I told you <u>about</u> the magazine.
  (2) We are proud <u>of</u> the pretty granddaughter.
  (3) Your great-grandfather was born <u>in</u> the town.
  (4) I reached the top of Mt. Mauna Kea <u>on</u> the day.

Endangered Species ❷ in the World
pp.60-61

1 (1) mass extinction
  (2) the Red List Categories
2 (1) 大量の   (2) 絶滅
  (3) 火山の   (4) 噴火
  (5) 完全に   (6) 生息地
  (7) 森林伐採   (8) 乱獲
  (9) 密猟する   (10) 範ちゅう，区分
  (11) 出版する
  (12) 驚かせる，不安にさせる

Nice Fit

were caused by volcanic eruptions

3 (1) the reason why you didn't go
  (2) Do you remember the day when we
  (3) I want to know the reason why
  (4) the day when I left
4 (1) is caused by
  (2) right now
5 (1) T
  (2) F
  (3) F
  (4) T

解説

3 次のように考えてみよう。
  (1) the reason に後ろから修飾節をつけるときは関係副詞 why を用いる。「あなたが行かなかった理由」は the reason why you didn't go とする。この際 why が省略されることもある。the reason が省略され，間接疑問文が続いているともとれる形 Tell me why you didn't go. とすることも多い。
  (2) Do you remember the day □□ we first met? 修飾節 we first met で空所の語は，「そのとき」という副詞の働きをして，先行詞 the day を修飾節でつないでいる。したがって時を表す関係副詞を入れる。
5 (2) F：WWF ではなく IUCN が発行。
  (3) F：65%ではなく80%が正しい。

1 (1) 50% of animals on the land of Japan (that inhabit only Japan)
　(2) 3,676 kinds of animals and plants

2 (1) 重大な　(2) 存在する
　(3) 生息する　(4) 省
　(5) コウノトリ　(6) ラッコ
　(7) ジュゴン　(8) メダカ
　(9) 庁　(10) (計画を)実行する
　(11) 人工的な　(12) 繁殖

Nice Fit

protect endangered species

3 (1) I visited the city where I lived when I was in Applause University
　(2) how we wash our hands
　(3) the town where I was born
　(4) how he lost weight

4 (1) not only, but also
　(2) and so on

5 (1) F
　(2) T
　(3) F
　(4) T

解説

3　次のように考えてみよう。
　(1) Recently I visited the city ☐ I lived when I was in Applause University.
　修飾節 I lived when I was in Applause University で空所の語は「その場所で，そこで」という副詞の働きをして，先行詞 the city と修飾節をつないでいる。したがって，場所を表す where を入れる。
　(2) how は関係副詞で「どうやって〜するかという方法」の意味である。This is how 〜で「これが〜する方法である」または「こうして〜する」という表現になる。

5 (1) F：日本だけではなく世界的な大問題。
　(3) F：植物だけではなく「動物」も含む。

---

1 (1) people
　(2) some animals

2 (1) 除外する　(2) 回復させる
　(3) 毛皮　(4) 設立する
　(5) 保護区域　(6) 異種交配する
　(7) 脅す　(8) 皮肉
　(9) 救う

Nice Fit

destroyed its habitats

3 (1) where
　(2) which
　(3) when
　(4) which

4 (1) was excluded from
　(2) worked well

5 (1) T
　(2) F
　(3) F
　(4) T

解説

3 (1) 先行詞：the village(場所)
　(2) 先行詞：a Thanksgiving party(事柄)
　(3) 先行詞：Saturday(時)
　(4) 先行詞：My cousin came back from Cairns(つまり，前の文全体)
　関係代名詞の「非制限用法」の例文として，次の英文を銘記しておくとよい。She had four sons, who became a doctor.(彼女には息子が4人いて，その全員が医者になった。)

4 (2) ここで使われている動詞 work(ed)は，便利な表現で，「本来の機能を存分に発揮する」という意味で用いられます。例文を見ておきましょう。These pills will work on you.(この薬はあなたに効くでしょう。)

5 (2) パンダの生息数はむしろ増えている。
　(3) サンクチュアリは「禁猟区」である。

Lesson 8 Endangered Species in the World まとめ ❺ pp.66-67

1 (1) million
(2) habitat
(3) mammal
(4) sanctuary
(5) die [decrease]

2 (解答例) There are about 8 million 7 hundred thousand living things that exist on earth now. Yet lots of animals are disappearing. IUCN listed 13,482 kinds of animals as endangered species in 2018.

3 (1) in which
(2) when
(3) why
(4) how

4 (1) is the day when I am least busy
(2) no reason why you should go there
(3) in the shade of a tree where it was cool

5 (1) ⓐ some   ⓑ our   ⓒ past
ⓓ one   ⓔ their   ⓕ right
ⓖ Red   ⓗ see
(2) ① and so on   ⑦ for example
(3) ② why   ③ when
⑤ where   ⑧ how
(4) 大量絶滅は外国だけでなく日本においても重大な問題である。
(5) it also means that they will disappear on earth
(6) ⓐ F   ⓑ T   ⓒ F

解説

3 (1) 前置詞 in を関係代名詞 which の前に移動させる。
(2) 先行詞：the days に when 節をつなぐ。
(3) 先行詞：the reason に why 節をつなぐ。
(4) 先行詞：(the way)が消失，よって how。

5 (6) ⓐ F：気候変動もその原因のひとつ。
ⓒ F：650億年ではなく6,500万年前。

Lesson 9 The Dream of Special ❶ Makeup pp.68-69

1 (1) "Yoda" and "Goblin"
(2) 下の写真が偽物のゴリラであるということ

2 (1) 戦争   (2) スクリーン
(3) 特別な   (4) 化粧，メーキャップ
(5) 視覚の   (6) 演劇
(7) 想像上の   (8) 生き物
(9) 下の   (10) 偽物の
(11) 場面
(12) 動物園の飼育係

Nice Fit

a fake gorilla

3 (1) stay home if it rains
(2) when I get home
(3) if it snows tomorrow
(4) unless you drink it now

4 (1) such as
(2) side by side

5 エ

解説

3 時制の鉄則：〈時〉節・〈条件〉節の中では，意味が未来であっても「現在形」を用いる。
(1) 不要な語(句)－will rain
(2) 不要な語(句)－will get
(3) 不要な語(句)－will snow
(4) 不要な語(句)－will drink

4 (1) 「B など，B のような A，A たとえば B」：A, such as B   本問のように，B は2個以上の名詞(oranges and lemons)を列挙することもある。
(2) 「(横に)並んで」：side by side   縦に並ぶ場合は，one behind the other となる。

5 質問の主旨は「特殊メークを施してゴリラ・スーツを製作した目的は？」なので，エの「ゴリラと飼育員との接触シーンがあり，実物のゴリラでは危険だから」が正解となる。

1 (1) human-like animals

(2) a mermaid wig

(3) to be a special makeup artist

2 (1) 現実, 事実   (2) 方法, 手順

(3) 一変させる   (4) 人魚

(5) レンズ   (6) 隠す

(7) まゆ毛   (8) ゴム

(9) かつら   (10) 帽子

(11) 前もって, あらかじめ

(12) (化粧品を)つける

(13) ～に沿って   (14) 額

(15) 混ぜる   (16) 端, 縁

Nice Fit

apply makeup on her entire face

3 (1) were

(2) came, would ask

(3) had, might go

(4) could write, knew

4 (1) in reality

(2) transformed, into

5 (1) T

(2) F

(3) F

(4) F

解説

3 仮定法過去の急所を反芻しておさえよう。
　一英語では, 現在の事実に反することや, 起
こりそうにないことを仮定する場合には, 現
在の話であっても if 節の動詞に過去形を使う。

(1) be → were 原則的には were だが,
口語では was も使われる。

(2) come → came

(3) have → had

(4) know → knew

5 (2) F：人魚は「女人」(『広辞苑』)である。

(3) F：セロテープではなく接着剤を用いる。

(4) F：アニメ・スクールでは学修できない。

1 (1) many special makeup artists

(2) English

(3) Dick Smith

2 (1) 芸術家   (2) 世界的に有名な

(3) アカデミー, 美術院

(4) 賞   (5) 理髪業, ヘアデザイン

(6) 記事   (7) 広く知られた

(8) 興味   (9) 返事

(10) B だけでなく A も

(11) 交換   (12) ハリウッド

Nice Fit

a magazine article about Dick Smith

3 (1) I wish he could drive a car

(2) I wish I could speak Garman well

(3) I wish I were a bird

(4) We wish we had a million dollars

4 (1) in advance

(2) as well as

(3) dream come true

5 イ

解説

3 現在の事実に反して「～だったらいいのに」
と願うような経験は誰しもあるだろう。現在
の事実に反することや起こりえないことに対
して「～だったらいいのに」と願望を表す際,
英語では wish の＋後ろの節に仮定法過去を
続ける。

(1) I wish ＋ he could drive...

(2) I wish ＋ I could speak...

(3) I wish ＋ I were...

(4) We wish ＋ we had...

4 (1) 「前もって, あらかじめ」：in advance

(2) 「B だけでなく A も」：A as well as B

(3) 「夢に見た通りのことが現実となること」
：a dream come true

5 「カズ・ヒロが俄然英語学習に燃え始めた
理由は？」—「スミス氏に質問し, 助言内容
を理解することができるように」

1 (1) the Academy Award
  (2) Kazu Hiro
  (3) the thing you want to do

2 (1) 映画　　　　(2) 指名する
  (3) 主な，主要な　(4) 俳優
  (5) 断る　　　　(6) 役割
  (7) そういうわけで〜
  (8) まるで〜であるかのような
  (9) 努力する　(10) 〜の存在を信じる
  (11) 集中する　(12) 情熱

Nice Fit

Don't be afraid of making mistakes

3 (1) talks as if he knew everything about
  (2) as if he were left-handed
  (3) as if he were a native

4 (1) was afraid of hurting
  (2) concentrate on

5 (1) T
  (2) T
  (3) T
  (4) T

解説

Nice Fit の英文に関して

Don't be afraid of making <u>mistakes</u>.（失敗することを恐れてはいけない）　この場合，文末の単語を必ず「複数形」にすること。そうすることによって一般性を与える。

3　日本語でも，「講釈師，（まるで）見てきたような嘘をつき」といった表現でたとえ話をすることがあるが，英語でそうした話をする際は，as if と仮定法を用いる。
  (1) 実際は知らない…　as if he knew …
  (2) 実際は左ききではない…　as if he were …
  (3) 実際は母語話者ではない…　as if he were

5　カズ・ヒロがアカデミー賞を受賞するまでの経緯を述べたものであるが，(1)〜(4)すべてが本文の内容と一致している。

1 (1) imaginary
  (2) mermaid
  (3) Hollywood
  (4) passion
  (5) decide

2 （解答例）　In 2018, Kazu Hiro won the Academy Award for Best Makeup and Hairstyling. When he was in senior high school, he sent a letter to Dick Smith. Kazu Hiro soon got a reply from Smith. At 26, his dream to work in Hollywood came true.

3 (1) had, could
  (2) were, would
  (3) were, would be
  (4) comes

4 (1) talks as if he knew everything
  (2) wish I had enough money
  (3) if it is not windy tomorrow morning

5 (1) ① could　　⑧ were
  (2) ② from　　⑪ on
  (3) ③ あなたは書くのと同じくらい上手に英語を話したり読んだりしますか。　⑥もしカズ・ヒロが断ったら，私はその役を引き受けるつもりはない。
  (4) This exchange of letters changed his life
  (5) came true
  (6) why
  (7) what
  (8) Don't be afraid of making mistakes
  (9) to, questions, advice

解説

5 (4) This exchange of letters changed his life.（直訳：この手紙にやりとりが彼の人生を変えた。）　日本語には「人間を主語にした言い方」が多い。一方，英語では「人間でないもの」を主語にして表現することが多い。

由美のメール

pp.78-79

1 (1) a son

2 (1) あいさつ

(2) ホッケー

(3) ナショナルホッケーリーグ

(4) ～を楽しみに待つ

Nice Fit

in advance

3 (1) fond of eating

(2) flying to

(3) to ride in

4 (1) would like to live

(2) in advance

(3) looking forward to going

5 (1) F

(2) T

(3) T

(4) F

解説

3 (1) 本問の fond という形容詞は，叙述用法では単独で使われず，「of＋名詞」という前置詞句を伴う。

(2) この文は現時点で決まっている予定について述べている。出発するのが「明朝早く」であり，すでに準備も整っている可能性が高い。このような状況では，現在進行形がよく使われる。

(3) 不定詞の「形容詞的用法」に着目する。

4 (1) 「～したいものだ」：would like to do ～

(2) 「～前に」：in advance　具体的な時間は直前に置く。

(3) 「～するのを待ち遠しく思う」：look forward to -ing

5 (1) 12月20日「まで」ではなく，12月20日「から」としたためられている。

(2) nervous ≒ worried と考えられる。

(3) そのように自己紹介している。

(4) NBA ではなく，NHL とある。

ホストファミリーからのメール

pp.80-81

1 (1) ice hokey

(2) a rabbit and a cat

2 (1) 貼りつける，〈ファイル・写真・書類などを〉添付する

(2) 親切な行為

Nice Fit

We have a favor to ask you

3 (1) during

(2) in

(3) until

4 (1) Thank you for

(2) attaching a photo

(3) tell me how to

5 (1) T

(2) T

(3) T

(4) F

6 (1) He wants to play ice hockey with her

(2) They are going to go watch an NHL game

(3) They have a rabbit and a cat

(4) She wants to know how to cook sukiyaki

解説

3 (1) during＋名詞句と while＋節を正確に使い分けよう。

(2) 前置詞は，went ではなく ice skating と関連するので，to ではなく in を使う。

(3) until と by を正確に使い分けよう。

5 (1) 本文3行目にそう書かれている。

(2) 由美はホストファミリーと一緒に NHL 観戦に行く予定になっている。

(3) ブラウン家は兎と猫を飼っている。

(4) 肉ジャガではなく，すき焼きである。

6 (1) 二人の共通の趣味（スポーツ）は何か。

(2) Let's go together! が示唆している。

(3) Actually, we have pets. がヒントに。

(4) We have a favor to ask you. が味噌。

21

1 (1) to take clean water into our bodies
(2) clean water to drink
2 (1) 浄化する
(2) 能力
(3) 不可欠の, 必須の
(4) 獲得する
(5) 干ばつ
(6) 粉

Nice Fit

the exercise capacity gets low

3 (1) understand what you say
(2) What is important to you is
(3) from what it was ten years ago
(4) believe what he told me
4 (1) consist of
(2) were in danger
5 イ

解説
3 関係代名詞 what は先行詞なしで用い,「～すること・もの」を表す。関係代名詞 what に導かれる節は「名詞節」である。つまり先行詞なしで「名詞の働きをするかたまり」となるので, 関係詞節の部分が, 文中で「主語」や「補語」,「目的語」,「前置詞の目的語」として働くことができる。
(1) what you say：目的語
(2) What is important to you：主語
(3) what it was ten years ago：前置詞 from の目的語
(4) what he told me：目的語
4 (1) 「～で構成されている」：consist of ～
(2) 「危険にさらされている」：in danger
〈比較せよ〉 You're in danger!（危ない！）
You're dangerous!（危険人物）
5 「発展途上国において健康を害する人が多い主たる原因は？」―川や池から汲んできた汚い水を飲まざるを得ないから（イ）。

1 (1) poly-glutamic acid
(2) green algae
2 (1) （災害などの）直後の時期
(2) 供給　　　(3) トラック
(4) 近くの　　(5) 論文
(6) ポリグルタミン酸
(7) 可能性を秘めた
(8) 報告書, 発言
(9) 試み　　(10) 誤り, しくじり
(11) スプーン 1 杯
(12) 藻, 藻類　(13) 凝固する
(14) 沈殿する

Nice Fit

trials and errors

3 (1) It was I that [who] sent my brother to her office yesterday.
(2) It was my brother that I sent to her office yesterday.
(3) It was to her office that I sent my brother yesterday.
(4) It was yesterday that I sent my brother to her office.
4 (1) succeeded in getting
(2) a spoonful of sugar
(3) flash
5 (1) F
(2) T
(3) T
(4) F

解説
強調構文：It is[was] ～ that ... の形で「～」の部分を強調した文を「強調構文」と呼ぶ。強調したい部分には,「主語」以外に,「目的語」や「副詞」, および「副詞の働きをする語句」を入れることもできる。
5 (1) 「飲めたらなあ！」と思っただけである。
(4) 病原微生物を含まず, 飲むのに適した水。

1 (1)　water from the unimaginably dirty rivers
　(2)　the people in developing countries
　(3)　Oda

2 (1)　ショックを受ける
　(2)　想像できないほど
　(3)　幼児　　　(4)　～で死ぬ
　(5)　下痢　　　(6)　提供する
　(7)　破産した
　(8)　独立した，自立した
　(9)　雇用，職がある状態
　(10)　除去する　　(11)　貧困

Nice Fit

for a low price

3 (1)　Travelling
　(2)　Feeling
　(3)　Entering
　(4)　Seeing

4 (1)　must keep on trying
　(2)　for free

5 (1)　F
　(2)　T
　(3)　F
　(4)　F

解説

※ Check it out yourself! 分詞構文の作り方
　元の英文：Though she lives near the sea, she cannot swim.
　① 接続詞を消す。
　② 前後の節で主語が同じならばそれを消す。
　③ 残った動詞を -ing 形に変える。完成：
Living near the sea, she cannot swim.

5 (1)　pleased ではなく shocked なので「F」
　(2)　1～2行目にそう書かれているので「T」
　(3)　水の無料供出は得策ではないので「F」
　(4)　政府開発援助 ODA は無関係なので「F」

1 (1)　the purifying powder
　(2)　female vendors（Polyglu Ladies）
　(3)　see people all over the world drink clean water

2 (1)　ますます　　　(2)　行商人
　(3)　ポリグルタミン酸の略称
　(4)　追加の，余分の　　(5)　貢献する
　(6)　経済的な
　(7)　心理的な，精神的な
　(8)　断言する
　(9)　達成する，（成功を）収める
　(10)　精力的な，エネルギッシュ
　(11)　確かに，絶対に

Nice Fit

the women's economic and psychological independence

3 (1)　show me how to use
　(2)　know how to reserve a seat
　(3)　taught the students how to swim
　(4)　don't know how to get to your house

4 (1)　was known as
　(2)　Thanks to
　(3)　as long as

5　エ

解説

※表現の幅を広げよう！
　「to＋動詞の原形」の前には，how 以外の疑問詞（what, who, which, when, where）も置くことができ，「疑問詞＋不定詞」の形で意味のかたまりを作ることができる。

3 (1)　「～の使い方」：how to use ～
　(2)　「～の予約の仕方」：how to reserve ～
　(3)　「泳ぎ方」：how to swim
　(4)　「～への行き方」：how to get to ～

4 (1)　「～として知られる」：be known as ～
　(2)　時に皮肉がこめられる thanks to ～
　(3)　「～するなら」：as long as ＋ S ＋ V

Lesson 10 — Purifying Powder まとめ

Lesson 10 **Purifying Powder まとめ**
pp.90-91

1 (1) drought (2) earthquake
 (3) poverty (4) useful
 (5) respect

2 (解答例) In Bangladesh, Oda was shocked to see the local people drink dirty water. He did not give them good and delicious water for free, but he sold the purifying powder for a low price. In this way, he created employment in developing countries all over the world.

3 (1) It was in Asahikawa that I saw the woman
 (2) What you need is a good
 (3) Entering the cafeteria, I saw a friend of mine eating
 (4) I taught him how to swim

4 (1) It, until, that
 (2) how to speak English
 (3) Staying, in Vancouver

5 (1) ① it was water purifying powder that he finally succeeded in developing
    ② Visiting Bangladesh, Oda was shocked to see the local people drink water from the unimaginably dirty rivers or use it for cooking
    ③ Letting them sell the powder, he also creates employment to eliminate poverty

解説
4 (1) not ～ until ... の強調
   not ～ until ...(…まで～しない，…になって初めて～する)という表現を「強調構文」で協調する場合，not until ... を is[was] と that の間に挿入する。

文法の まとめ **文構造，時制，助動詞，受け身**
pp.92-93

1 (1) 3，アンはかわいい人形を作った。
 (2) 4，アンは彼に新しい帽子を作った。
 (3) 5，アンは彼を幸せにした。
 (4) 3，ゴードンはその本を簡単に見つけた。
 (5) 5，ゴードンはその本が易しいとわかった。

2 (1) turn (2) have broken
 (3) has lost または had given
 (4) belong (5) been

3 (1) should not
 (2) will not
 (3) have to または ought to
 (4) they should
 (5) used to または would often

4 (1) The door was closed by the doctor.
 (2) Is French spoken in Canada?
 (3) Daddy was not helped by Jane.
 (4) A bird has been killed by the dog.
 (5) A new covered bridge is being built over the river.

5 (1) Kirara is helping her mother in the kitchen.
 (2) They kept the door open. または They left the door open.
 (3) Yoshio is often praised by the teacher.
 (4) She didn't have to do such a thing. または She shouldn't have done such a thing.
 (5) COVID-19 will soon be eradicated.

解説
   注意すべき「過去の行動に対する後悔や非難の表現」(助動詞＋have＋過去分詞)
should[ought to] have＋過去分詞
「～すべきだったのに(実際はしなかった)」
shouldn't[ought not to] have＋過去分詞
「～すべきではなかったのに(実際はした)」
needn't have＋過去分詞
「～する必要はなかったのに(実際はした)」

24

1 (1)　Lake Biwa is larger than any other lake in Japan.
(2)　No other girl in our school is as [so] tall as Dunk.
(3)　This book is less difficult than that.
(4)　He is the cleverest boy in our class.
(5)　No other story I have ever read is as [so] amusing as this.

2 (1)　Did you hear her sing?
(2)　He was seen to cross the street.
(3)　You had better not go out in such a rain.
(4)　I must get him to copy this report.
(5)　I will have him carry the baggage upstairs.

3 (1)　Look at the dancing girl.
(2)　She lent me a book written in German.
(3)　The goods ordered last month...
(4)　The tree standing near the gate...
(5)　A barking dog seldom bites.

4 (1)　Seeing her son, she shouted with joy.
(2)　Not feeling well, I stayed at home all day.
(3)　Having finished my work, I had nothing to do.
(4)　It being a dull meeting, I left as soon as I could.
(5)　Judging from his accent, he must be an Australian.

5 (1)　He is not as tell as she is. [her]
(2)　Mt. Fuji is the highest mountain in Japan.
(3)　We can hear the bell ring at noon every day.
(4)　I had my picture taken by a friend of mine.
(5)　Judging form look of the sky, it will snow in the afternoon.

1 (1)　あなたに会うのはいつもとても楽しみです。　名詞
(2)　私に何か冷たい飲みものをください。 形容詞
(3)　彼女は音楽を学ぶためにイタリアへ行った。　副詞
(4)　私はその知らせを聞いてとても驚いた。 副詞
(5)　ピエール・カルダンは98歳まで生きた。 副詞

2 (1)　I found it difficult to read the Bible through. または …read through the Bible.
(2)　All you have to do is to do your best.
(3)　Have you decided where to build your house yet?
(4)　Not a star was to be seen in the sky.
(5)　She was kind enough to show me the way.

3 (1)　help［stop］彼の黄色いネクタイには笑わざるを得ないよ。　　(2)　like あの晩彼女は外出する気分ではなかった。　　(3)　no 君とは議論しても埒が明かない。
(4)　without 健康が富に勝るのは言うまでもない。　　(5)　prevented [stopped, kept] 病気のため昨日はパーティーに出られませんでした。

4 (1)　lending　(2)　reading
(3)　smoking
(4)　to mail　(5)　seeing

5 (1)　To tell the truth, I don't like dogs.
(2)　This tea is too hot to drink.
(3)　I don't feel like studying math tonight.
(4)　I don't think this article is worth reading.
(5)　Aren't you ashamed for having said such a thing?

関係代名詞・関係副詞・条件節・仮定法　pp.98-99

1 (1) If Taka weren't in bad health, he could study hard.

(2) I wish you were here.

(3) If you had not gotten angry, she wouldn't have gone out of the room.

(4) If he had not been busy, he could have been [gone] there.

(5) If it had not rained last night, the read would not be bad now.

2 (1) 彼が正直なら，私は彼を雇う。

(2) もし彼が正直なら，私は彼を雇うのに。

(3) 彼がここに来たら，そう伝えるよ。

(4) 私は彼がここにいつ来るのか知らない。

(5) 私は明日雨が降るかどうか知らないが，もし雨が降ったら私は家にいます。

3 (1) Hyuma is the boy whose father is a professional baseball player.

(2) The man who is reading a newspaper is my uncle.

(3) A planet is a star which [that] moves around the sun.

(4) I bought this dictionary, which helped me a lot.

(5) Mitsuru has a new car which [that] he is very proud of.

4 (1) This is place where I lost my digital single-lens reflex camera.

(2) I went over the garden, where she was sitting under a tree.

(3) Nobody knew the reason why the lights went out.

(4) The time when your dream will come true will come. ／ The time will come when your dream will come true.

(5) This is the way we wash our faces out of doors.

5 (1) If you had come five minutes earlier, you would not have missed the bus.

(2) She behaves as if she were a boy.

(3) If he comes, let's go to the concert together.

(4) Toshiko has an uncle who [that] works for a bank.

(5) Tuesday is a day when he is very busy.

解説

命名「仮定法ミックス」

〜「（過去に）もし…だったら，（現在は）…だろう」の言い表し方〜

　例文1　If she had studied in Australia, her English would be quite different now.（もしオーストラリアに留学していたら，今の彼女の英語はまったく違っているだろう。）

　例文2　If he hadn't started cricket at the age of 6, he wouldn't be such a good player now.（彼がもし6歳でクリケットを始めていなかったら，今これほどよい選手にはなっていないだろう。）

　例文1では，if節には had studied という仮定法過去完了が使われており，「（あの時）〜だったら」と過去の事実に反する仮定を述べている。主節では would be という仮定法過去に対応する形が使われており，現在のことについて「〜だろう」と話している。このように，「（過去に）もし〜だったら，（現在は）…だろう」と仮定する場合には，if節に仮定法過去完了を用い，主節には，仮定法過去に対応する（would be といった）「助動詞の過去形＋動詞の原形」を用いることになる。例文2は否定文のケースである。

　さて，この仮定法の用例には名前がまだない。手元の文法書，参考書を見ても例外として扱っているものがほとんどのようだ。そこで提案である。どうであろうか，この用法を「仮定法ミックス」と呼んでみては。

総合問題 **1**

pp.100-106

1 〈リスニング問題〉

A (1) ウ　　(2) ウ

B (1) ウ　　(2) イ　　(3)エ

音声スクリプト

A.

(1)

W : Would you like to go to a wheelchair basketball game with me next Saturday?

M : Yes, I'd like to. When and where shall we meet?

W : It starts at 4:00. So let's meet at the station at 3:30.

M : At the station at 3:30. All right, fine.

(2)

M : How did you do on your Japanese history test, Kate?

W : Not bad. It was much easier than I thought. How about you, Mark?

M : I didn't do so well. I had a severe headache last night, so I couldn't study very much.

W : I didn't know that. That's too bad.

音声スクリプト

B.

Mary has two pen pals, one in Australia and the other in Japan. Last week, she got a picture postcard from Australia. It was from Patty in Melbourne. In the picture people were enjoying skiing. Mary got a letter from her Japanese friend, Yasuko, almost at the same time. In the picture sent by Yasuko, people were bathing in the sea. Mary was surprised to find that her two pen pals were living in totally opposite seasons.

〔要約〕　メアリーにはペンフレンドが二人いる。

一人はオーストラリアのパティー，もう一人は日本のヤスコ。先週その二人からほぼ同時期に便りがあった。パティーから届いた絵はがきの写真はスキー(真冬)で，ヤスコが同封してくれた写真は海水浴(真夏)だったので，メアリーはあらためて地球の大きさと広さに感じ入った。

2

(1) イ

(2) エ

(3) イ

(4) ウ

(5) エ

(6) ア

(7) イ

(8) ウ

(9) ウ

(10) ア

3

(1) ウ

(2) ア

(3) イ

(4) ウ

(5) エ

(6) イ

4

(1) grandmother bought, Thursday

(2) too, for, to

(3) Have, ever read

(4) found, injured

(5) named me, calls me

(6) was, doing

(7) haven't seen [met], for

(8) found, easily

(9) bought, for her

(10) written by

5

(1) ① ウ ② カ ③ イ

(2) ⓐ オーストラリア ⓑ 豆腐

(3) エ

6

(1) ウ

(2) A ア B ウ C イ

(3) ⓐ 他人［だれかほかの人］

ⓑ 1番 ⓒ 楽しむ

(4) ウ

7

(1) イ

(2) エ

(3) ③ イ ④ オ

(4) 私たちは海にどれくらいの数の生物が生息しているかわからない。

(5) ウ と エ

総合問題 **2**

1 〈リスニング問題〉

A (1) イ (2) エ

B (1) エ (2) ウ (3) ア

音声スクリプト

A.

(1)

W : Excuse me. How far is it from here to the Dinosaur Museum? I'm thinking of walking there.

M : Oh, the museum is too far from here. If you walk one block that way, you can catch the bus.

W : Do the buses run often?

M : They run every 15 minutes or so in the daytime.

(2)

M : Susie, I just heard about the "Azalea" charity marathon in May. Let's do it.

W : But I'm not a fast runner like you.

M : That's not important. I'm sure running through fresh green leaves will make us feel good.

W : I don't know. Let me think about it.

音声スクリプト

B.

Jeff works as an aircraft mechanic at an airline company. His enormous workload makes him very busy. Recently he has been feeling stressed at work. When he talked to Carolyn, one of his co-workers, about his problem, she suggested that he should try dog therapy with her. Jeff thought it might be a good idea, and he is going to visit the therapy center for the first time this weekend. His mental health needs some maintenance. He has to keep himself in good condition by checking or repairing it regularly just like an aircraft engine.

〔要約〕 ジェフは航空会社で飛行機の整備士をしている。最近仕事が忙しく，ストレスを感じていた。ジェフは自分の精神状態を会社の同僚のキャロラインに相談すると，「ドッグ・セラピー」なるものを紹介してくれたうえに，一緒に来てくれるという。ジェフは今度の週末にセラピー・センターに行ってみるつもりだ。職場の航空機のエンジンと同じように，彼の心も定期点検とメンテナンスが必要なのかもしれない。メンタル・ヘルスも良い状態を維持したいものだ。

2
- (1) イ
- (2) ウ
- (3) イ
- (4) エ
- (5) エ
- (6) ア
- (7) ア
- (8) エ
- (9) ウ
- (10) イ

3
- (1) ウ
- (2) ウ
- (3) ア
- (4) ウ
- (5) イ
- (6) エ

4
- (1) sent, living, April
- (2) cousin, good swimmer
- (3) as old as
- (4) had to, could solve
- (5) could you
- (6) will, able, in
- (7) hotter, than
- (8) if, is
- (9) If, had, could finish
- (10) wish, could, speak

5
- (1) ① オ　② キ　③ ア　④ ウ
- (2) ⓐ ニューヨーク　ⓑ シカゴ
- (3) エ

6
- (1) ① ウ　② エ
- (2) ア
- (3) ア
- (4) ⓐ 経験　ⓑ 発見
- (5) イ

7
- (1) 私は自分にどの職業がいちばんよいのかわからなかった。
- (2) ⓐ 将来　ⓑ 友人
- (3) ウ
- (4) ア
- (5) イ, オ

1〈リスニング問題〉

A （1）ア　　（2）イ

B （1）エ　　（2）イ　　（3）ウ

音声スクリプト

A.

(1)

W：Why were you absent from school yesterday, Hans?

M：I've got a terrible toothache.

W：That's too bad. You'd better see a dentist as soon as possible.

M：You're right. I've got an appointment this afternoon.

(2)

M：(The phone rings. 電話音入る) Hello. This is George speaking. May I talk to Kirara?

W：Kirara speaking. Hi, George. How are you doing?

M：Fine. Do you want to go to a concert on Sunday?

W：I'm sorry I can't. I'm going to a flea market with Hina.

音声スクリプト

B.

(The chimes ring. 校内放送のチャイム鳴る) Good morning! Attention, all students. Today there will be a whole school assembly in the gym beginning at 1:35. Please bring a notebook and a pen, as we will be explaining university applications and the various steps that need to be taken from now until graduation. As a reminder, the University Fair is coming up next week on Friday at the Civic Plaza. All students and parents are invited to attend. A list of universities participating in the University Fair will be handed out at the end of today's assembly. Thank you.

〔要約〕（ピンポンパンポ〜ン！）全校生徒に連絡します。本日午後１時35分より本校体育館において全校集会を行います。ノートとペンを持参するように。——大学入試の出願手続き方法の説明，および卒業までの重要な連絡と諸注意を行いますのでメモするように。参考までに，来週の金曜日，市民プラザにおいて大学フェアが実施される予定です。保護者同伴で参加できます。どういった大学が参加するかのリストを本日の集会終了後に配布いたします。以上。（ピ〜ンポンパンポン！）

2

(1)　ウ

(2)　ウ

(3)　エ

(4)　イ

(5)　エ

(6)　エ

(7)　ア

(8)　ウ

(9)　エ

(10)　ア

3

(1)　イ

(2)　エ

(3)　イ

(4)　ア

(5)　イ

(6)　ウ

4

(1)　have much, August

(2)　May, ask, of

(3)　sister, good pianist

(4)　can't, as [so] well as

(5)　let me watch

(6)　looking forward to visiting

(7) give me something hot to drink

(8) which [that] you lent me

(9) whose windows

(10) where you can see

5

(1) ① エ　　② イ
　　③ オ　　④ ア

(2) ⓐ　2　　ⓑ　日　　ⓒ　前

6

(1) ① イ　　② ウ　　③ ア

(2) ウ

(3) ⓐ　父親　　ⓑ　20ドル紙幣
　　ⓒ　落とした

(4) イ

7

(1) ⓐ　将来就きたい職業　　ⓑ　料理学校
　　ⓒ　料理

(2) 彼は皿洗いをしているときに，ときどき
他の料理人がしていることを見た。

(3) ウ

(4) ウ

(5) ア

ここまでがんばってくれた君へ
　その努力に賞賛の拍手(applause)を送りま
す。applause は可算名詞として使われること
のない純粋の抽象名詞としての運命を背負って
います。したがって形容詞に修飾されても不定
冠詞は付かない —— ×a loud applause —— の
です。その熱き抽象性を懐深く秘めて，次年度
の A P P L A U S E 　 E N G L I S H
COMMUNICATION II に進んでください。
You can do it!　　　　　　　　　　　(H)

APPLAUSE

ENGLISH COMMUNICATION I
WORKBOOK

解答・解説

開隆堂出版株式会社
東京都文京区向丘 1-13-1

BC

英語は「語順が命」です。

SV SVC SVO

英文は主に S（主語）・V（動詞）・O（目的語）・C（補語）の 4 つの要素で構成されます。

Many people look at this picture.
 S   V

補語（C）は主語（S）を説明する。S＝Cの関係になるんだよね。

They are really **impressive**.
 S V   C

We sometimes **see these pictures**.
 S   V O

目的語（O）は動詞が表す動作や状態の対象を表す。「～を，～に」という意味ね。

3 【文法】日本語に合う英文になるように，（　　）内の語句を並べかえましょう。

(1) 祖母はいなかに住んでいる。　(the country / my grandmother / in / lives).

_____.

(2) あのビルは非常に高い。　(high / is / very / that building).

_____.

(3) 私は彼女の歌が好きだ。　(her / I / songs / like).

_____.

(4) 妹はピンク色の服を着てかわいらしく見えた。

(looked / my sister / her pink dress / pretty / in).

_____.

4 【表現】日本語に合う英文になるように，￣￣￣から適切な語を選んで空所に書きましょう。

(1) 彼女は母親のようには料理ができません。

She can't cook _____ her mother does.

(2) 彼はお茶を一杯召し上がりたいんじゃないかしら。

He _____ like _____ have a cup of tea, I think.

to	like	would

5 【内容理解】本文の内容に合うように，次の質問に対する適切な答えをア～エから選びましょう。

What do people probably want to do when they see these beautiful pictures?　（　　　）

ア　They want to look at some more pictures.

イ　They want to read guidebooks.

ウ　They want to visit these places.

エ　They want to make artificial islands.

I like to go to the library.

1 【本文理解】音声を聞いて，区切りに気をつけて音読し，下の問いに答えましょう。

In Japan, / we also have many places / with beautiful scenery. //
        S   V   O

Look at this picture. // It is Mt. Fuji, / a World Heritage Site, / in the spring. // Mt. Fuji /

and its reflection in the lake / look beautiful / with cherry blossoms. //

Look at this amazing view. // These are / the ruins of Takeda Castle / in Hyogo

Prefecture. // There is a sea of clouds / around the ruins. // ❶They look wonderful, / and

the view / looks like a painting. //

   G These pictures give us / peace of mind. // However, / the beautiful scenery is
               S   V   O   O

changing / because some people / don't care about the environment. // What do you

think / about ❷that? //

(1) 下線部❶ They は何を指すのか，文中の語句で答えましょう。 _____

(2) 下線部❷ that はどのような事態を指すのか，日本語で簡潔に書いてみよう。 _____

2 【単語】次の語句の意味を調べて書きましょう。

(1) heritage* 名(   )   (2) site* 名(   )

(3) cherry blossom(s)* 名(   )   (4) reflection 名(   )

(5) ruin(s) 名(   )   (6) castle* 名(   )

(7) prefecture* 名(   )   (8) painting 名(   )

(9) peace* 名(   )   (10) mind* 名(   )

(11) care 動(   )   (12) environment* 名(   )

Nice Fit 本文から抜き出しましょう。

逆さ富士＝(   )(   )(   )(   )(   )

Coffee Break

reflection（お尻につけて動詞から名詞に）
-tion のように，お尻につけて動詞から名詞になるものには，下記のようなものがあります。
-ment, -ance, -age, -al, -y ここで，辛い recollection(思い出)を1つ。初めて渡米した際，喫茶店で
コーヒーと一緒にアップルパイを注文したら，ホールで出てきたことがありました。

英会話
footwork

What kind of TV programs do you like to watch?

Grammar

SVOO

目的語を２つとる場合，「人」を表す間接目的語と「物」を表す「直接目的語」とに区別されます。
SVOO の文では，「相手（〜に）」と「もの（〜を）」を示す２つの目的語を置きます。

These pictures **give us peace of mind**.
    S   V   O   O

The teacher sometimes **shows students beautiful paintings**.
  S   V   O   O

> １つ目の O には「受け取る人」，２つ目の O には「受け取るもの」がくるのね。

> 「人に・ものを」の第４文型と覚えよう。give と buy がよく使われるよ。

3 【文法】日本語に合う英文になるように，（　　）内の語句を並べかえましょう。

(1) 私は妹に人形をあげた。　(a doll / my sister / gave / I).

_____.

(2) 彼女は昨日フレディーに CD をあげた。　She (Freddie / yesterday / gave / a CD).

She _____.

(3) 父は私に新しい辞書を買ってくれた。　(me / bought / new dictionary / a / my father).

_____.

(4) 彼らは私たちに駅へ行く道を教えてくれた。　They (the way / showed / the station / us / to).

They _____.

4 【表現】日本語に合う英文になるように，[　　]から適切な語を選んで空所に書きましょう。

(1) 彼女は有能な女性のようだ。

She _____ _____ an able woman.

(2) 彼らが何と言おうと気にしない。

I don't _____ _____ what they say.

about	looks	care	like

5 【内容理解】本文の内容に合う文は T を，合わない文は F を○で囲みましょう。

(1) We have many places with beautiful scenery in Japan. 　　　　　　　　（ T / F ）

(2) Mt. Fuji will be a World Heritage Site soon. 　　　　　　　　　　　　（ T / F ）

(3) The ruins of Takeda Castle are in Hyogo Prefecture. 　　　　　　　　（ T / F ）

(4) The beautiful scenery is not changing because everybody cares about the environment.

　　　　　　　　　　　　　　　　　　　　　　　　　　　　　　　　　　（ T / F ）

> I like to watch *anime*.

1 【本文理解】音声を聞いて，区切りに気をつけて音読し，下の問いに答えましょう。

Japan has four seasons, / and we enjoy nature / with the seasons. //

Sei-Shonagon wrote / about the four seasons / in *Makura-no-Soshi*, / (*The Pillow
Book*). // "In spring, / dawn is the best time, / because it is breaking / slowly and
gradually. // In summer, / nights are good, / because fireflies / are flitting about. // In fall, /
the sunset is good, / because crows go back / to **❶**their nests. // And in winter, / snowy
early mornings / are the best." //

　G We find / the change of the seasons / very useful. // But now, / **❷**it is disappearing /
because the climate is changing. // What do you think / about that? //

(1) 下線部**❶** their は「誰／何の～」という意味か，日本語で答えましょう。　＿＿＿＿＿

(2) 下線部**❷** it は何を指すのか，文中の語句で答えましょう。　＿＿＿＿＿

2 【単語】次の語句の意味を調べて書きましょう。

(1)	pillow	名(	)	(2)	dawn	名(	)
(3)	break*	動(	)	(4)	gradually	副(	)
(5)	fireflies < firefly	名(	)	(6)	flitting < flit	動(	)
(7)	sunset*	名(	)	(8)	crow(s)	名(	)
(9)	nest*	名(	)	(10)	useful*	形(	)
(11)	disappear*	動(	)	(12)	climate*	名(	)

Nice Fit 本文から抜き出しましょう。

四季の移り変わり ＝(　　　　)(　　　　)(　　　　)(　　　　)(　　　　)

Coffee Break

「保護」か「補語」か，それが問題・田(だ)。
ハワイでタロイモの水田を見学しようとしたとき，ガイドさんに "You'll find the plantation fallow." と
言われたことがあります。fallow はそう頻繁に目にする単語ではありませんが，「(地質を保護するために)
休耕中」という意味の形容詞です。この英文，まさに S＋V＋O＋C から成り立っていたのでした。

英会話 footwork

What kind of food do you like to eat?

Grammar

SVOC

O＝C の関係が成立し，「O を C にする・だとわかる」などの意味になります。

We find the change of the seasons very useful.
  S   V   O   C

Four seasons make Japan a beautiful country.
    S   V   O   C

> 補語 (C) は目的語 (O) を説明しているんだね。

> この文型では，make，name，keep などがよく使われるわ。

3 【文法】日本語に合う英文になるように，（　　）内の語句を並べかえましょう。

(1) 彼らは子どもにロームという名前をつけた。　(their / Rome / they / child / named).

  _____.

(2) その知らせを聞いて彼女は幸せになった。　(happy / her / the news / made).

  _____.

(3) 彼らは最初の子どもにジョージという名前をつけた。

(their / they / George / first child / named).

  _____.

(4) その知らせを聞いて彼は悲しくなった。　(made / the / sad / news / him).

  _____.

4 【表現】日本語に合う英文になるように，▢▢▢から適切な語を選んで空所に書きましょう。

(1) 日本は四季がはっきりしている。

The _____ _____ are clear in Japan.

(2) 彼は明日関空からホノルルに帰ります。

He is _____ _____ to Honolulu from Kansai Airport tomorrow.

seasons	back	going	four

5 【内容理解】本文の内容に合うように，次の質問に対する適切な答えをア〜エから選びましょう。

According to Sei-Shonagon, when is the best time in winter?　　　　　　（　　　）

ア　Dawn is the best time, because it is breaking slowly and gradually.

イ　Nights are good, because fireflies are flitting about.

ウ　The sunset is good, because crows go back to their nests.

エ　Snowy early mornings are the best.

> I like to eat Italian food.

7

1 【英語定義】次の英語の定義に相当する英単語を書きなさい。　　　　〈5点×5〉

(1) not natural or real, made by the art of man　　　　_____

(2) large area of water enclosed by land　　　　_____

(3) soft cushion for the head, especially when lying in bed　　　　_____

(4) display of colored light, mainly red and green, seen in the sky　　　　_____

(5) learn by heart　　　　_____

2 【ストーリー・リテリング】教科書 p.18 (Section 3) を4回音読した後，次の語句をすべて用いて本文を自分の言葉で再現しなさい。　　　　〈10点〉

[使用語句]：four seasons, nature, Sei-Shonagon, change, climate

_____

_____

_____

3 【文法】日本語に合う英文になるように，（　　）内の語句を並べかえなさい。　　　　〈5点×4〉

(1) なぜあなたはそんなにうれしそうなのか。　　(you / happy / so / look / do / why)?

_____?

(2) 彼女は私に郵便局への道を教えてくれた。

(the / she / way / showed / to / me) the post office.

_____ the post office.

(3) その男は彼女を幸せにした。　　(man / made / the / her / happy).

_____.

(4) 机の上に地図があります。　　(map / the desk / there / a / is / on).

_____.

4 【文法】日本語に合う英文になるように，空所に適切な語を書きなさい。　　　　〈6点×3〉

(1) 彼女はその知らせを聞いて青くなった。

She _____ _____ to hear the news.

(2) 私の父は市の中心部で中華料理店を経営している。

My father _____ a Chinese restaurant _____ the center of the city.

(3) 彼は息子を一人ぼっちにしておいた。

He _____ his son _____.

5 【内容理解】次の英文を読んで，下の問いに答えなさい。　　　　　　　　〈計27点〉

①There are many places (　　　) beautiful scenery in the world. We sometimes see these pictures. They are really impressive. Look at this picture. This is an aurora with various colors. It is amazing. It is a natural light display, and it is like a beautiful light show in the sky. These are heart-shaped islands. They are romantic. They are not artificial islands. When people see these pictures, they probably want to visit these places. ②(to / these / you / places / visit / like / would)?

In Japan, we also have many places with beautiful scenery. Look at this picture. It is Mt. Fuji, a ③_____ _____ Site, in the spring. ④Mt. Fuji and its reflection in the lake look beautiful with cherry blossoms. Look at this amazing view. These are the ruins of Takeda Castle in Hyogo Prefecture. There is a sea of clouds around the ruins. They look wonderful, and the view looks like a painting. These pictures give us peace of mind. However, the beautiful scenery is changing because some people don't care about the environment. What do you think about that?

Japan has ⑤_____ _____, and we enjoy nature with the seasons. Sei-Shonagon wrote about the four seasons in *Makura-no-Soshi*, (*The Pillow Book*). "In spring, dawn is the best time, because it is breaking slowly and gradually. In summer, nights are good, because fireflies are flitting about. In fall, the sunset is good, because crows go back to their nests. And in winter, snowy early mornings are the best." ⑥We find the change of the seasons very useful. But now, it is disappearing because the climate is changing. What do you think about that?

(1) 下線部①の(　　　)に入る適切な語を ☐ から選んで書きなさい。　　　　　　(2点)

in	for	at	with

＿＿＿＿＿＿＿＿

(2) ②の(　　　)内の語を並べかえて，「こういった場所に行ってみたいですか。」という意味になるようにしなさい。　　　　　　　　　　　　　　　　　　　　　　　　　　(4点)

＿＿＿＿＿＿＿＿＿＿＿＿＿＿＿＿＿＿＿＿＿＿＿＿＿＿＿＿＿＿＿＿＿＿ ?

(3) ③が「世界遺産」，⑤が「四季」という意味になるように， ☐ から適切な語を選んで書きなさい。　　　　　　　　　　　　　　　　　　　　　　　　　　　　　　　(3点×2)

③＿＿＿＿＿＿ ＿＿＿＿＿＿　　　⑤＿＿＿＿＿＿ ＿＿＿＿＿＿

seasons	World	four	Heritage

(4) 下線部④を日本語にしなさい。　　　　　　　　　　　　　　　　　　　　　　(5点)

＿＿＿＿＿＿＿＿＿＿＿＿＿＿＿＿＿＿＿＿＿＿＿＿＿＿＿＿＿＿＿＿＿＿＿＿＿＿

(5) 下の文が下線部⑥の意味を表すように，⑦，④の空所に適切な日本語を補いなさい。　(3点×2)
私たちには⑦(　　　　　　　　)が④(　　　　　　　　　　)であるということがわかります。

(6) 本文の内容に合うように，次の質問に対する適切な答えを完成させなさい。　　(4点)
Why is the beautiful scenery is changing?
——Because some ＿＿＿＿＿＿ don't ＿＿＿＿＿＿ ＿＿＿＿＿ the ＿＿＿＿＿ .

1 【本文理解】音声を聞いて，区切りに気をつけて音読し，下の問いに答えましょう。

You may think of chocolate / as a sweet solid food / for everyone. // A long time ago, / however, / **①**<u>it</u> was a non-sweet drink / only for rich people. // **G** They thought / that it

　　　　　　　　　　　　　　　　　　　　　　　　　　　　 S 　　　　 V 　　(接続詞) S′

gave them energy. // In the 16th century / of the Aztec Empire, / the Emperor

V′　 O′　　O′

Montezuma / drank 50 cups of chocolate / a day. //

　Chocolate is made / from cacao beans. // One cacao pod contains / 30 to 40 beans. // In

　　　　　　　　　　　　　　　　　　　　　 S　　　 V　　　　　 O

those days, / **②**<u>they</u> were so precious / that people used them / as a currency. // People

paid one grain / for a large tomato. // They called cacao / "the food of the god." //

(1) 下線部**①** it は何を指すのか，文中の語で答えましょう。　　　　　　　＿＿＿＿＿＿

(2) 下線部**②** they は何を指すのか，文中の語句で答えましょう。　　　　　＿＿＿＿＿＿

2 【単語】次の語句の意味を調べて書きましょう。

(1) mysterious	形(　　　　　　)	(2) solid	形(　　　　　　)
(3) Aztec	形(　　　　　　)	(4) empire	名(　　　　　　)
(5) emperor	名(　　　　　　)	(6) Montezuma	名(　　　　　　)
(7) cacao	名(　　　　　　)	(8) bean(s)	名(　　　　　　)
(9) pod	名(　　　　　　)	(10) contain(s)	動(　　　　　　)
(11) currency	名(　　　　　　)	(12) grain	名(　　　　　　)

Nice Fit 本文から抜き出しましょう。

通貨として用いた＝(　　　　　) (　　　　　) (　　　　　) (　　　　　) (　　　　　)

Coffee Break

a <u>sweet</u> <u>solid</u> food（形容詞の語順）

形容詞がいくつか重なる場合は，修飾される名詞に関係が深いもの（sweet よりも solid）ほどその名詞の近くにおかれるのが原則です。だいたいは次の語順に従います。

①大小＋②形状＋③性質・状態＋④色彩＋⑤年齢・新古＋⑥材料・固有形容詞

おっと，雨が降り出しました。Where is my <u>black</u> <u>folding</u> umbrella? I must have misplaced it.

英会話 footwork

What country would you like to visit in the future?

SVO（that 節）

〈that＋S＋V〉のかたまりで「〜ということ」という意味になります。

「〜ということ」という意味の that は省略することもできます。

They thought 〈that it gave them energy〉.

I know 〈that chocolate is made from cacao beans〉.

 that が導く節が目的語（O）の働きをしているのね。

 節というのは〈S＋V〉を含む語句のまとまりのことで，that は「S が V するということ」のようにまとめる働きをしているんだ。

3 【文法】日本語に合う英文になるように，teach, hear, know, say のうちの1語を適切な形にかえて空所に書きましょう。

(1) 彼女は私たちに詩を読むのは楽しいということを教えてくれた。

She ＿＿＿＿＿＿ ＿＿＿＿＿＿ ＿＿＿＿＿＿ reading poetry was fun.

(2) だれもが地球が丸いということを知っている。

Everyone ＿＿＿＿＿＿ ＿＿＿＿＿＿ the earth is round.

(3) 来年新しい音楽の先生が私たちの学校に来るそうです。

I ＿＿＿＿＿＿ ＿＿＿＿＿＿ we will have a new music teacher next year.

(4) 弟は台湾については何でも知っていると言っています。

My brother ＿＿＿＿＿＿ ＿＿＿＿＿＿ he knows everything about Taiwan.

4 【表現】日本語に合う英文になるように，□□□から適切な語を選んで書きましょう。

(1) ワインはぶどうから作られる。

Wine ＿＿＿＿＿＿ ＿＿＿＿＿＿ ＿＿＿＿＿＿ grapes.

(2) 当時は，たいていの人がテレビを持っていなかった。

＿＿＿＿＿＿ ＿＿＿＿＿＿ ＿＿＿＿＿＿, most people didn't have TV.

those	made	is	in	from	days

5 【内容理解】本文の内容に合う文は T を，合わない文は F を○で囲みましょう。

(1) A long time ago, chocolate was something non-sweet to drink only for rich people.

(T / F)

(2) In the 16th century, the Emperor Montezuma drank fifteen cups of chocolate a day.

(T / F)

(3) One cacao pod contains 30 to 40 beans. (T / F)

(4) They called cacao beans "the food for thought." (T / F)

I'd like to visit Australia.

1 【本文理解】音声を聞いて，区切りに気をつけて音読し，下の問いに答えましょう。

In 1521, / the Spanish conquered / the Aztec Empire. // At first, / ❶they hated
　　　　　S　　　　　　V　　　　　O
chocolate / because it tasted / bad to them. // However, / after they brought it to Europe, /

noble people began to drink it / with sugar. // It refreshed them so much / and became

G more popular / than coffee or tea. //
　　(比較級)

In 1847, / the great invention came / when a British company mixed chocolate / with

cocoa butter / instead of hot water. // ❷It changed chocolate / from drink / into a solid
　　　　　　　　　　　　　　　　　　　　　S　　V　　　　　　　O
food. // It spread beyond rich people / and to ordinary people / all over the world. // The
　　　　S　　V
present style of chocolate / is fairly new / historically. //
　　　　S　　　　　　V　　　　C

(1) 下線部❶ they は誰を指すのか，文中の語句で答えましょう。　　　　　　　　　_____

(2) 下線部❷ It は何を指すのか，文中の語句で答えましょう。　　　　　　　　　　_____

2 【単語】次の語句の意味を調べて書きましょう。

(1) the Spanish*　　　名(　　　　　　)　(2) conquer(ed)　　動(　　　　　　)

(3) at first*　　　　　(　　　　　　)　(4) hate*　　　　　　動(　　　　　　)

(5) noble　　　　　形(　　　　　　)　(6) refresh(ed)　　　動(　　　　　　)

(7) invention*　　　名(　　　　　　)　(8) cocoa　　　　　名(　　　　　　)

(9) butter　　　　　名(　　　　　　)　(10) instead of ~*　　(　　　　　　)

(11) beyond　　　　前(　　　　　　)　(12) historically　　　副(　　　　　　)

Nice Fit 本文から抜き出しましょう。

固形食物 ＝(　　　　　　)(　　　　　　)(　　　　　　)

Coffee Break

conquer(頭につけていっしょの仲間)
con- のように，単語の語頭につくものとして，下記のようなものがあります。
co-, syn-, sym-, cor-, col-

英会話
footwork

Which season do you like the best?

Grammar

比較①

比較級:〈比較級(語尾に er をつける)+than〉で「～よりも…だ」という意味になります。

単語が長いときなどは,語尾に er をつけずに more を単語の前に置きます。

The present style of chocolate is sweeter <u>than</u> chocolate in the 16th century.
～よりも甘い

It became <u>more popular than</u> coffee or tea.
～よりも人気がある

〈-er+than〉で「より～」,〈the+-est〉で「最も～」の意味だよ。

比較的長い形容詞や副詞(3音節以上)には more(比較級)をつけるのよ。

3 【文法】日本語に合う英文になるように,(　　)内の語を適切な形にかえて空所に書きましょう。

(1) ぼくは岩男さんより体重がある。

I am _____ than Iwao-san. (heavy)

(2) 四国はハワイ諸島より少しだけ大きい。

Shikoku is a little _____ than the Hawaiian Islands. (large)

(3) タブレットは以前より子どもたちに普及しています。

Tablet is _____ _____ among children than before. (popular)

(4) この古い道具はあの新しいのより役に立ちます。

This old tool is _____ _____ than that new one. (useful)

4 【表現】日本語に合う英文になるように,□□□から適切な語を選んで書きましょう。

(1) 彼は仕事に行かず1日中寝ていた。

He stayed in bed all day _____ _____ going to work.

(2) 伊保子は世界中で知られている有名な科学者です。

Ihoko is a famous scientist known _____ _____ _____ _____.

| over | of | world | all | instead | the |

5 【内容理解】本文の内容に合うように,次の質問に対する適切な答えをア～エから選びましょう。

How did they change chocolate from drink into a solid food?　　　　　　(　　　)

ア　The Spanish conquered the Aztec Empire in 1521.

イ　Noble people in Europe began to drink chocolate with sugar.

ウ　Chocolate became more popular than coffee or tea in Britain.

エ　A British company mixed chocolate with cocoa butter instead of hot water.

I like fall the best.

1 【本文理解】音声を聞いて，区切りに気をつけて音読し，下の問いに答えましょう。

> In Japan, / the Dutch brought a chocolate beverage / to Dejima in Nagasaki / in the
> late 18th century. // At that time, / ❶it was a rare drink / from overseas. // After that, / it
> spread gradually / throughout Japan, / and now / it is / one of **G** the most popular
> (最上級)
> sweets. //
>
> In addition to that, / chocolate is getting popular / as healthy food. // Scientific studies
> show / that cacao polyphenol / in chocolate / is good for the health. // For example, / ❷it
> lowers blood pressure. //
>
> Look at the chart. // Dark chocolate has / about four times / **G** as much polyphenol /
> as an apple. // Chocolate is / a really interesting food. //
> (同等比較)

(1) 下線部❶ it は何を指すのか，文中の語句で答えましょう。　＿＿＿＿＿＿＿＿

(2) 下線部❷ it 何を指すのか，文中の語句で答えましょう。　＿＿＿＿＿＿＿＿

2 【単語】次の語句の意味を調べて書きましょう。

(1) the Dutch 名( )	(2) beverage 名( )
(3) rare 形( )	(4) overseas 副( )
(5) spread* 動( )	(6) throughout 前( )
(7) in addition to 〜* ( )	(8) scientific 形( )
(9) polyphenol 名( )	(10) health 名( )
(11) lower(s) 動( )	(12) chart 名( )

Nice Fit 血圧を下げる ＝( )( )( )

Coffee Break

電話英会話の４重要ポイント
① Speak loudly!　② Speak clearly!　③ Don't hesitate to speak!
④ Write down the message!
さあ，心を開いて電話英会話をエンジョイしましょう！
The mind is like an umbrella. It's most useful when open.
（精神《マインド》は傘のようなものだ。開いているとき，一番使い道がある。）

英会話 footwork

What do you like to do when the weather is cold?

比較②

最上級：〈the＋最上級（語尾に -est）＋of [in]〜〉で「〜でもっとも…」という意味になります。

as 〜 as …：２つのものが同じ大きさ・程度であることを表します。

It spread gradually throughout Japan, and now it is one of <u>the most</u> popular sweets.
1番人気がある

Dark chocolate has about four times <u>as</u> much polyphenol <u>as</u> an apple.
〜の４倍のポリフェノールを

〈the＋-est〉あるいは〈the most＋比較的
長い形容詞や副詞〉で「最も〜」の意味ね。

〈as＋原級＋as〉で「同じくらい〜」の
意味だよ。

3 【文法】日本語に合う英文になるように，（　　）内の語を適切な形にかえて空所に書きましょう。

(1) ハンスは私の弟と同じくらい早く走れる。

Hans can run ＿＿＿＿＿ ＿＿＿＿＿ ＿＿＿＿＿ my brother.　(fast)

(2) ２月はすべての月の中で一番短い。

February is ＿＿＿＿＿ ＿＿＿＿＿ ＿＿＿＿＿ all the months.　(short)

(3) この滝は私たちの街の中で最も有名です。

This waterfall is ＿＿＿＿＿ ＿＿＿＿＿ ＿＿＿＿＿ in our town.　(famous)

(4) 英語は外国人とコミュニケーションをとる上で最も重要である。

English is ＿＿＿＿＿ ＿＿＿＿＿ ＿＿＿＿＿ in communicating with foreign people.

(important)

4 【表現】日本語に合う英文になるように，□□□から適切な語を選んで空所に書きましょう。

(1) 夏目漱石はよい小説家であるばかりでなく，偉大な学者でもあった。

＿＿＿＿＿ ＿＿＿＿＿ ＿＿＿＿＿ being a good novelist, Natsume Soseki was a great

scholar.

(2) 例えば看護師のように夜勤をしなければならない人も多い。

Many people — ＿＿＿＿＿ ＿＿＿＿＿, nurses — have to work at night.

in	example	to	addition	for

5 【内容理解】本文の内容に合う文は T を，合わない文は F を○で囲みましょう。

(1) The Dutch brought chocolate bars to Dejima in Nagasaki in the late 18th century.（T / F）

(2) In Japan, a chocolate beverage spread at a very quick pace.　　　　　　　　（T / F）

(3) Scientists say that sugar in chocolate is good for the health.　　　　　　　（T / F）

(4) Dark chocolate has about four times as much polyphenol as a cup of black coffee.（T / F）

I like to stay home.

1 【英語定義】次の英語の定義に相当する英単語を書きなさい。　〈5点×5〉

(1) money that is actually in use in a country　＿＿＿＿＿＿

(2) sweet substance used in cooking and for sweetening tea, coffee, and so on　＿＿＿＿＿＿

(3) slowly, little by little, by degrees, over a long period of time　＿＿＿＿＿＿

(4) substance (powder or drink) made from the crushed seeds of the cacao tree　＿＿＿＿＿＿

(5) be fond of　＿＿＿＿＿＿

2 【ストーリー・リテリング】教科書 p.30 (Section 3) を 4 回音読した後，次の語句をすべて用いて本文を自分の言葉で再現しなさい。　〈8点〉

[使用語句]：the Dutch, the 18th century, sweets, addition, healthy

＿＿＿＿＿＿＿＿＿＿＿＿＿＿＿＿＿＿＿＿＿＿＿＿＿＿＿＿＿＿＿＿＿＿＿＿＿＿

＿＿＿＿＿＿＿＿＿＿＿＿＿＿＿＿＿＿＿＿＿＿＿＿＿＿＿＿＿＿＿＿＿＿＿＿＿＿

＿＿＿＿＿＿＿＿＿＿＿＿＿＿＿＿＿＿＿＿＿＿＿＿＿＿＿＿＿＿＿＿＿＿＿＿＿＿

3 【文法】日本語に合う英文になるように，（　）内の語を並べかえなさい。　〈5点×4〉

(1) 東京は日本で最大の都市です。　Tokyo (Japan / largest / is / in / city / the).

Tokyo ＿＿＿＿＿＿＿＿＿＿＿＿＿＿＿＿＿＿＿＿＿＿＿＿＿.

(2) 由衣は糸よりピアノがうまい。　Yui (plays / than / piano / better / the) Ito.

Yui ＿＿＿＿＿＿＿＿＿＿＿＿＿＿＿＿＿＿＿＿＿＿＿ Ito.

(3) 困ったことに彼はパスポートを失くした。

The trouble is (has / passport / he / his / that / lost).

The trouble is ＿＿＿＿＿＿＿＿＿＿＿＿＿＿＿＿＿＿＿＿＿＿＿.

(4) 時間ほど価値のあるものはない。　Nothing (as / time / valuable / as / is).

Nothing ＿＿＿＿＿＿＿＿＿＿＿＿＿＿＿＿＿＿＿＿＿＿＿.

4 【文法】日本語に合う英文になるように，適切な語を空所に書きなさい。　〈6点×3〉

(1) 私はいとこほど歳をとっていない。

I'm ＿＿＿＿＿ ＿＿＿＿＿ ＿＿＿＿＿ ＿＿＿＿＿ my cousin.

(2) 私は彼がいつか外国へ行きたいと思っていることを知っている。

I ＿＿＿＿＿ ＿＿＿＿＿ he ＿＿＿＿＿ ＿＿＿＿＿ go abroad someday.

(3) 彼女は彼女の妹よりも美しい。

She is ＿＿＿＿＿ ＿＿＿＿＿ ＿＿＿＿＿ her sister.

5 【内容理解】次の英文を読んで，下の問いに答えなさい。　　　　　　〈計27点〉

You may think of chocolate as a sweet solid food for everyone. A long time ago, however, it was a non-sweet drink only for rich people. They thought that it gave them energy. In the 16th century of the Aztec Empire, the Emperor Montezuma drank 50 cups of chocolate a day.

Chocolate is made from cacao beans. One cacao pod contains 30 to 40 beans. ①In those days, they were so precious that people used them as a currency. People paid one grain for a large tomato. They called cacao "the food of the god."

In 1521, the Spanish conquered the Aztec Empire. ②_____ _____, they hated chocolate because it tasted bad to them. However, after they brought it to Europe, noble people began to drink it with sugar. It refreshed them so much and became ③(much) popular than coffee or tea.

In 1847, the great invention came when a British company mixed chocolate with cocoa butter instead of hot water. It changed chocolate from drink into a solid food. It spread beyond rich people and to ordinary people all over the world. The present style of chocolate is fairly new historically.

In Japan, the Dutch brought a chocolate beverage to Dejima in Nagasaki in the late 18th century. At that time, it was a rare drink from overseas. After that, it spread gradually throughout Japan, and now it is one of the ④(much) popular sweets.

In addition to that, chocolate is getting popular as healthy food. Scientific studies show that cacao polyphenol in chocolate is good for the health. ⑤_____ _____, it lowers blood pressure.

Look at the chart. ⑥Dark chocolate has about four times as much polyphenol as an apple. Chocolate is a really interesting food.

(1) 下線部①を they および them が何を指すのかを明らかにして，日本語にしなさい。　(7点)

_____

(2) ②が「最初は」，⑤が「たとえば」という意味になるように，☐☐☐から適切な語を選んで書きなさい。
　　②_____ _____　　　⑤_____ _____　　(3点×2)

| For | In | At | possibility | example | first |

(3) ③，④の（　）内の語を適切な形にかえて書きなさい。　　　　　　　(2点×2)
　　③_____　　　④_____

(4) 下線部⑥の意味を表すように，㋐，㋑の中に適切な日本語を補いなさい。　(3点×2)
　　ブラックチョコレートには，リンゴ1個のおよそ㋐(　　　　　　)の㋑(　　　　　　)が含まれている。

(5) 本文の内容に合う文はTを，合わない文はFを○で囲みなさい。　　　　(2点×3)
　　ⓐ　A long time ago, chocolate was a non-sweet drink only for rich people. 　　(T / F)
　　ⓑ　A Spanish company mixed chocolate with cocoa butter instead of hot water.

　　　　　　　　　　　　　　　　　　　　　　　　　　　　　　　　　　(T / F)
　　ⓒ　According to scientific studies, caffeine in chocolate is good for the health. 　(T / F)

17

1 【本文理解】音声を聞いて，区切りに気をつけて音読し，下の問いに答えましょう。

In Japan, / many students play sports / in school clubs. // ❶They usually play / only one
_S _V _O

sport. // Of course, / this idea has some merits. // However, / in the U.S., / club activities in
_S _V _O

high school / have a season system, / so many students there / practice different sports. //

For example, / some students play soccer / from September to December, / basketball /
_S _V _O _O

from January to March, / and tennis / from April to June. //
_O

This system / is not familiar to Japan, / but young students' participation / in multiple

sports / **G** has been an important topic / in the U.S. / for a long time. // What do you
(現在完了形)

think / of ❷this new idea? //

(1) 下線部❶ They は誰を指すのか，文中の語句で答えましょう。　　　　　　　_____

(2) 下線部❷ this はどのようなものか，日本語で簡潔に答えましょう。　　　　　_____

2 【単語】次の語句の意味を調べて書きましょう。

(1) school club* 名( ) (2) usually* 副( )

(3) of course* 副( ) (4) idea* 名( )

(5) merit(s) 名( ) (6) however* 副( )

(7) system* 名( ) (8) practice* 動( )

(9) for example* 副( ) (10) familiar 形( )

(11) participation 名( ) (12) multiple 形( )

Nice Fit 本文から抜き出しましょう。

シーズン制を採用している ＝( )( )( )( )

☕ **Coffee Break**

demerit(頭につけて前進・反対思いのまま)
demerit の de- のように，頭につけて「前進・反対」の意味になるものに，下記ようなものがあります。
de-, ab-, se-, dis-, contra-, contro-, counter-, anti-, ante-, pro-, pre-

英会話 footwork

When did you start studying English?

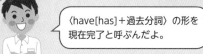

Grammar

現在完了形

〈have[has]＋過去分詞〉を現在完了形といいます。

「継続」用法：「(今までずっと)～しています」

「経験」用法：「(今までに)～したことがあります」

「完了・結果」用法：「(もう・すでに)～してしまいました」

Young students' participation in multiple sports

<u>has been</u> an important topic in the U.S.

Many students in America <u>have practiced</u> different sports.

I <u>have</u> already <u>finished</u> swimming practice today.

> 〈have[has]＋過去分詞〉の形を現在完了と呼ぶんだよ。

> 現在完了形は過去と現在をつなぐ線(LINE)とも言えますね。現在完了の意味を考えるとき、4つのK(経験, 継続, 結果, 完了)が大切ね。

---

3 【文法】日本語に合う英文になるように，（　　）内の語句を並べかえましょう。

(1) 私はカナダに2回行ったことがある。　(to / have / Canada / twice / been / I).

_____.

(2) 彼は休暇でバリ島へ行ってしまった。　He(to / on / has / vacation / gone / Bali).

He _____.

(3) 彼女は1週間学校を休んでいる。　She(absent / school / been / from / has)for a week.

She _____.

(4) 私は5年前から彼を知っている。　I(him / five / have / for / years / known).

I _____.

---

4 【表現】日本語に合う英文になるように，□□□から適切な語を選んで空所に書きましょう。

(1) その山の名前はよく知っている。

The name of the mountain _____ _____ _____ me.

(2) 私のアイディアをどう思いますか。

_____ _____ _____ _____ _____ my idea?

| do | think | is | what | you | familiar | to | of |

---

5 【内容理解】本文の内容に合う文はTを，合わない文はFを○で囲みましょう。

(1) A lot of students in Japan play sports in school clubs. （ T / F ）

(2) Many Japanese students usually play only one sport. （ T / F ）

(3) In the U.S., many students practice multiple sports. （ T / F ）

(4) In Japan, club activities in high school have a season system. （ T / F ）

> I started studying English in junior high school.

19

The Secrets of Top Athletes

Lesson 3 — Section 2 ▶pp.40-41

1 【本文理解】音声を聞いて，区切りに気をつけて音読し，下の問いに答えましょう。

Multiple sports / have many advantages / for young people. //
S V O

First, / young students acquire / various abilities / through multiple sports
S V O
experiences. // For example, / when students play basketball, / ❶they improve / their
decision-making skills and muscle endurance. // These abilities are useful / when they
play other sports. //

Second, / multiple sports experiences / enable young students / to build their bodies /
and decrease / the chance of injury. //

Some students in Japan / G have been playing / the same sport / since an early age. //
S V(現在完了進行形) O
In this case, / the possibility of injury / increases / because repetitive movements / strain
❷their body / and possibly affect / the development of muscles. //

(1) 下線部❶ they は誰を指すのか，文中の語で答えましょう。 _____
(2) 下線部❷ their は誰を指すのか，文中の語句で答えましょう。 _____

2 【単語】次の語や語句の意味を調べて書きましょう。

(1) advantage* 名(　　　) (2) acquire 動(　　　)
(3) experience* 名(　　　) (4) improve 動(　　　)
(5) muscle 名(　　　) (6) endurance 名(　　　)
(7) enable 動(　　　) (8) possibility 名(　　　)
(9) repetitive 形(　　　) (10) strain 動(　　　)
(11) affect* 動(　　　) (12) development 名(　　　)

Coffee Break

development（お尻につけて動詞から名詞）
development の -ment のように，単語のお尻につけて動詞から名詞になるものに，下記のようなものがあります。
-ment, -tion, -ance, -age, -al, -y

20　　英会話 footwork　　What kind of books do you like to read?

Grammar

現在完了進行形

〈have[has] ＋been＋動詞の ing 形〉を現在完了進行形といいます。

過去のある時点から現在まで「動作」が続いていることを表します。

Some students in Japan <u>have been playing</u> the same sport since an early age.

My dogs <u>have been running</u> since they arrived at the park.

> 現在までずっと〜し(続け)ているというダイナミックな意味ね。

> 動作の継続を表すには，現在完了進行形〈have[has] been＋〜ing〉を用います。

Nice Fit 本文から抜き出しましょう。

筋肉の発育＝（ 　　　　　 ）（ 　　　　　 ）（ 　　　　　 ）（ 　　　　　 ）

3 【文法】日本語に合う英文になるように，空所に適切な語を書きましょう。

(1) 私の弟たちは今まで14時間眠り続けている。

My brothers _____ _____ _____ _____ fourteen hours.

(2) うちの息子は１時間ずっと電話で話をしている。

My son _____ _____ _____ _____ the phone for an hour.

(3) 先週からずっと雨が降り通しだ。

It _____ _____ _____ _____ last week.

(4) 日本の「はやぶさ２」は2014年からずっと飛行を続けている。

Japan's Hayabusa 2 spacecraft _____ _____ _____ _____ 2014.

4 【表現】日本語に合う英文になるように，□□□から適切な語を選んで空所に書きましょう。

(1) リカコの言葉で，水に対する恐怖に打ち克つことができた。

Rikako's words _____ me _____ overcome my fear of water.

(2) グレースは幼いころから海辺にすんでいます。

Grace has lived by the sea _____ _____ _____ _____.

| age | early | an | since | to | enabled |

5 【内容理解】本文の内容に合うように，次の質問に対する適切な答えをア〜エから選びましょう。

Why does the possibility of injury for some students in Japan increase?　　　（ 　　 ）

ア　Because they improve their decision-making skills and muscle endurance.

イ　Because they have been playing different sports since an early age.

ウ　Because they acquire various abilities through multiple sports experiences.

エ　Because repetitive movements strain their body and affect the development of muscles.

> I like to read books about history.

1 【本文理解】音声を聞いて，区切りに気をつけて音読し，下の問いに答えましょう。

Many top athletes / in the world / are good at multiple sports. // So are / some Japanese
athletes. // Kiyomiya Kotaro, / a professional baseball player, / had been a swimmer / and
a rugby player / before he played baseball. // He says, / "I loved swimming and rugby /
when I was a small child." // So he didn't quit ❶them / because of baseball. //

And Shibuno Hinako, / a popular professional golfer, / **G** had been a softball player /
（過去完了形）
before she played golf. // Thanks to her experiences / in playing softball, / she has
improved at golf. // In 2019, / ❷she won / the Women's British Open Golf Tournament. //

Some top athletes / have trained themselves / through various experiences. // Not only
top athletes / but also any of us / can improve ourselves / when we try / various things. //

(1) 下線部❶ them は何を指すのか，文中の語句で答えましょう。　＿＿＿＿＿＿

(2) 下線部❷ she は誰を指すのか，文中の語句で答えましょう。　＿＿＿＿＿＿

2 【単語】次の語句の意味を調べて書きましょう。

(1) be good at ～*　　（　　　　）　(2) swimmer　　名（　　　　）

(3) quit　　動（　　　　）　(4) because of ～*　　（　　　　）

(5) popular*　　形（　　　　）　(6) professional　　形（　　　　）

(7) golfer　　名（　　　　）　(8) golf　　名（　　　　）

(9) thanks to ～*　　（　　　　）　(10) train*　　動（　　　　）

(11) improve*　　動（　　　　）　(12) tournament　　名（　　　　）

Nice Fit 本文から抜き出しましょう。

人気プロゴルファー＝（　　　　）（　　　　）（　　　　）（　　　　）

Coffee Break

professional（お尻につけて名詞から形容詞）
professional の -nal のように，お尻につけて名詞から形容詞になるものに，下記のようなものがあります。
-al, -ous, -ic, -y, -ful, -able, -ive, -ible, -ish, -ly

英会話 footwork

Which do you like better, studying at home or at the library?

過去完了形

〈had＋過去分詞〉を過去完了形といいます。

過去完了は〈had＋過去分詞〉で表すんだ。

「継続」用法：「(そのときまでずっと)〜していました」

「経験」用法：「(そのときまでに)〜したことがありました」

過去完了形を用いた文では、過去のどの時が基準となっているかに注意することが大切ね。

「完了・結果」用法：「(そのときまでにもう・すでに)〜してしまっていました」

Shibuno Hinako, a popular professional golfer, <u>had been</u> a softball player before she played golf.

Otani Shohei <u>had visited</u> the U.S. before he became a major leaguer.

Kiyomiya Kotaro <u>had become</u> famous until he became a high school student.

3 【文法】日本語に合う英文になるように，(　　)内の語を並べかえましょう。

(1) 彼は彼女から借りた傘をなくした。

He lost the umbrella that (he / from / her / borrowed / had).

He lost the umbrella that _____ .

(2) 私は逗子に引っ越すまでここに住んでいた。

I (lived / here / had / I / before) moved to Zushi.

I _____ moved to Zushi.

(3) 彼女は亡くなるまで雪を見たことがなかった。　She (never / had / seen) snow till she died.

She _____ snow till she died.

(4) 私が帰宅したときには，もう雨はやんでいた。

The rain (stopped / already / had) when I got home.

The rain _____ when I got home.

4 【表現】日本語に合う英文になるように，☐☐から適切な語を選んで空所に書きましょう。

(1) シェイクスピアは作家というだけではなく，役者でもあった。

Shakespeare was _____ _____ a writer _____ _____ an actor.

(2) クリケットの競技経験はありますか。

Do you have any _____ _____ _____ cricket?

only	also	experiences	not	but	playing	in

5 【内容理解】本文の内容に合う文はTを，合わない文はFを○で囲みましょう。

(1) Some professional athletes have trained themselves through various experiences. (T / F)

(2) Kiyomiya Kotaro had been a skier and a rugby player before he played baseball. (T / F)

(3) Shibuno Hinako had been a soft tennis player before she played golf. (T / F)

(4) Ordinary persons cannot improve themselves when they try various things. (T / F)

At home. The library is too far from my house.

The Secrets of Top Athletes

1 【英語定義】次の英語の定義に相当する英単語を書きなさい。 〈5点×5〉

(1) common, usual, often seen or heard, well known to _____

(2) game, played by 2 teams of 5 players who try to throw a large ball into a net _____

(3) person who is good at running, jumping, swimming, boxing, and so forth _____

(4) make or become greater in size, number, degree, and the like _____

(5) put up with _____

2 【ストーリー・リテリング】教科書 p.40（Section 2）を4回音読した後，次の語句をすべて用いて本文を自分の言葉で再現しなさい。 〈8点〉

[使用語句]：multiple sports, young people, first, second, injury

_____

_____

_____

3 【文法】日本語に合う英文になるように，適切な語を空所に書きなさい。 〈5点×4〉

(1) 私は傘をなくしてしまいました。

_____ _____ _____ my umbrella.

(2) 私たちは引っ越す以前，埼玉に住んでいた。

We _____ _____ _____ Saitama before we moved.

(3) 彼女は私がその自転車を買ったことを知らなかった。

She didn't know that _____ _____ _____ the bike.

(4) その赤ちゃんはほとんど10分泣き通しです。

The baby _____ _____ _____ for almost ten minutes.

4 【文法】日本語に合う英文になるように，（　）内の語を並べかえなさい。 〈5点×4〉

(1) 私は台湾を訪れたことがない。 I (been / have / Taiwan / to / never).

I _____.

(2) 彼女は昨日まで病気で寝ていた。 She (sick / bed / in / been / had) until yesterday.

She _____ until yesterday.

(3) 彼は2年間バイオリンをひいている。 He (violin / been / has / the / playing) for two years.

He _____ for two years.

(4) あなたはパリに来てどのくらいになりますか。 (you / Paris / how / in / long / been / have)?

_____?

5 【内容理解】次の英文を読んで，下の問いに答えなさい。 〈計27点〉

Multiple sports have many advantages for young people.

First, young students acquire various abilities through multiple sports experiences. For example, when students play basketball, they improve their decision-making skills and muscle endurance. These abilities are useful when they play other sports.

Second, ①(build / students / to / multiple sports experiences / their bodies / young / enable) and decrease the chance of injury.

Some students in Japan have been playing the same sport since an early age. ②_____ _____ _____, the possibility of injury increases because repetitive movements strain their body and possibly affect the development of muscles.

Many top athletes in the world are good at multiple sports. ③So are some Japanese athletes. Kiyomiya Kotaro, a professional baseball player, ④(be) a swimmer and a rugby player before he played baseball. He says, "I loved swimming and rugby when I was a small child." So he didn't quit them because of baseball.

And Shibuno Hinako, a popular professional golfer, had been a softball player before she played golf. ⑤_____ _____ her experiences in playing softball, she has improved at golf. In 2019, she won the Women's British Open Golf Tournament.

Some top athletes have trained themselves through various experiences. ⑥Not only top athletes but also any of us can improve ourselves when we try various things.

(1) 下線部①の（　　）内の語句を並べかえて，「多様なスポーツを経験することによって，若い学生は体力をつけることができる。」という意味にしなさい。 (4点)

（　　　　　　　　　　　　　　　　　　　　　　　　　　　　　　　　　　　　　）

(2) ②が「こういった場合には」，⑤が「～のおかげで」という意味になるように，□□□から適切な語を選んで書きなさい。 (3点×2)

② _____ _____ _____　　⑤ _____ _____

Effect	In	Thanks	On	to	from	here	case	this

(3) 下線部③とほぼ同じ意味になるように，次の空所に適語を書きなさい。 (4点)

Some Japanese top athletes _____ _____ _____ multiple sports, _____.

(4) ④の（　　）内の語の適切な形をア～オから選んで記号を書きなさい。 (3点)

ア be　　イ is　　ウ was　　エ has been　　オ had been （　　　）

(5) 下線部⑥を日本語にしなさい。 (5点)

_____

(6) 本文の内容に合うように，次の質問に対する適切な答えを完成させなさい。 (5点)

Why does the possibility of injury increase if some students in Japan have been playing the same sports since an early age?

——Because _____ _____ strain their body and possibly affect the _____ _____ _____.

25

Lesson ④ Evolving Airplanes

1 【本文理解】音声を聞いて，区切りに気をつけて音読し，下の問いに答えましょう。

Since ancient times, / humans have been dreaming / of flying in the sky. // After various challenges, / finally, / the Wright brothers, / Wilbur Wright and Orville Wright, /
s
G could fly a manned airplane / on December 17th, / 1903. // Its name was Wright
v   **o**
(助動詞)
Flyer. // **❶**It had / a gasoline engine and two propellers. // This was the very first flight / in
s v   **c**
history. // Orville Wright / flew about 36.5 meters / in 12 seconds. // **❷**It was a great step /
s v   **c**
for humankind. // Since then, / airplanes have developed greatly / and evolved / in various ways. //

Now, / an airplane **G** can fly / more than ten thousand kilometers / and carry / more
(助動詞)
than five hundred people. //

(1) 下線部❶ It は何を指すのか，文中の飛行機名で答えましょう。　　　＿＿＿＿＿＿

(2) 下線部❷ It は何を指すのか，日本語で簡潔に答えましょう。　　　＿＿＿＿＿＿

2 【単語】次の語句の意味を調べて書きましょう。

(1) evolve　　　　　　　動(　　　　　)　　(2) airplane(s)　　　名(　　　　　)

(3) ancient*　　　　　　形(　　　　　)　　(4) finally*　　　　　副(　　　　　)

(5) manned　　　　　　形(　　　　　)　　(6) Wright Flyer　　名(　　　　　)

(7) gasoline　　　　　　名(　　　　　)　　(8) propeller(s)　　　名(　　　　　)

(9) the very first ～*　　　(　　　　　)　　(10) flight　　　　　　名(　　　　　)

(11) humankind　　　　　名(　　　　　)

Nice Fit 本文から抜き出しましょう。

史上初飛行＝(　　　　) (　　　　) (　　　　) (　　　　) (　　　　) (　　　　)

Coffee Break

propeller（頭につけて前進・反対思いのまま）
propeller の pro- のように，頭につけて前進や反対の意味になるものに，下記のようなものがあります。
pro-, pre-, anti-, ante-, contra-(contrast：教科書 p.95), contro-, counter-, ab-, de-, se-, dis-

英会話
footwork

Have you ever traveled abroad?

助動詞

動詞の原形の前に置かれ，動詞にさまざまな意味を付け加えます。

can / could：can は「能力」「可能性」，could は「過去の能力」「推量」を表します。

ほかに，may, might, must, have to, should, ought to などがあります。

An airplane <u>can</u> fly more than ten thousand kilometers.

主語が「3人称単数現在」でも -s や -es を付けないんだ。

助動詞は，動詞の原形の前に置いて，いろいろな意味を付け加える言葉ね。

3 【文法】日本語に合う英文になるように，空所に can，may，must のいずれかを書きましょう。

(1) ボブはフランス語をとても上手に話すことができます。

Bob _____ speak French very well. 〈参考〉Bob is able to speak French very well.

(2) あなたはあしたレポートを書かなければなりません。

You _____ write a report tomorrow. 〈参考〉You have to write a report tomorrow.

(3) この本を家へ持ち帰ってもよろしいでしょうか。

_____ I take this book home? 〈参考〉Can I take this book home?

(4) 彼女は間違っているかもしれない。

She _____ be wrong.

〈参考〉There is a possibility that she is wrong but this is not certain.

4 【表現】日本語に合う英文になるように，□□□から適切な語を選んで空所に書きましょう。

(1) これは一人の人間にとっては小さな一歩だが，人類にとっては偉大な一歩である。

That's one _____ _____ for a man, one _____ leap for mankind.

(2) 子供はさまざまな仕方で成長する。

Children develop _____ _____ _____.

| ways | step | in | small | various | giant |

5 【内容理解】本文の内容に合う文は T を，合わない文は F を○で囲みましょう。

(1) Since ancient times, humans have been dreaming of going skydiving. （T / F）

(2) Wilbur Wright and Orville Wright were distant cousins. （T / F）

(3) The Wright brothers were able to fly a manned airplane more than a century ago. （T / F）

(4) The name of the very first airplane in history was Wright Flight. （T / F）

(5) Now, an airplane can carry more than five hundred passengers. （T / F）

Yes. I went to New Zealand last summer.

1 【本文理解】音声を聞いて，区切りに気をつけて音読し，下の問いに答えましょう。

What will airplanes be like / in the future? // One company is planning / to invent a new type of airplane. // The airplane will not have / any windows. // The walls and the
S   V   O
ceiling / will be the screens. // The airplane has / exterior cameras. // The passengers can see /
S   V
the outside scenery / on the screen. // This type of airplane / uses fewer materials, / so / **❶**it
O
is lighter. //

New types of engines / will use bio-fuels, / electricity, / or solar energy. // **❷**They will be eco-friendly / and won't make much noise. // **G** The speed is expected / to be Mach 4.5, / or
(受動態)
5,500 kilometers per hour. // We will be able to enjoy / a convenient and comfortable
S   V
flight. //
O
Airplanes are developing / and evolving / day by day. //

What can you imagine / future airplanes might look like? //

(1) 下線部**❶** it は何を指すのか，文中の語句で答えましょう。 _____

(2) 下線部**❷** They は何を指すのか，文中の語句で答えましょう。 _____

2 【単語】次の語句の意味を調べて書きましょう。

(1) company*   名(   )   (2) invent*   動(   )

(3) ceiling   名(   )   (4) exterior   形(   )

(5) passenger(s)   名(   )   (6) bio-fuel(s)   名(   )

(7) electricity*   名(   )   (8) solar*   形(   )

(9) eco-friendly   形(   )   (10) noise*   名(   )

(11) Mach   名(   )   (12) per   前(   )

Nice Fit 本文から抜き出しましょう。

今後，将来＝(   )(   )(   )

Coffee Break

exterior(頭がエキスパーとで外に出る)

exterior の ex-(外に出る)のように，頭につけるものに，下記のようなものがあります。

ex-, ec-, es-, super-, sur-

英会話
footwork

Are you a member of any clubs?

• Grammar

受動態

〈be 動詞＋過去分詞〉で「…される」という受動態（受け身）の意味になります。

The speed <u>is expected</u> to be Mach 4.5, or 5,500 kilometers per hour.

A manned airplane <u>was made by</u> the Wright brothers.

> be 動詞が is / am / are なら「…され（てい）る」，was / were なら「…され（てい）た」の意味になるのよ。

> 〈be 動詞＋過去分詞〉で「…され（てい）る」という受け身の意味を表すんだね。

3 【文法】日本語に合う英文になるように，（　　）内の動詞を適切な形にかえて空所に書きましょう。

(1) グリーン先生はどの生徒にも好かれています。　(like)

Mr. Green ＿＿＿＿＿＿ ＿＿＿＿＿＿ ＿＿＿＿＿＿ every student.

(2) 私は昨日パーティーに招待されませんでした。　(invite)

I ＿＿＿＿＿＿ ＿＿＿＿＿＿ to the party yesterday.

(3) 彼女は先生にしかられましたか。　(scold)

＿＿＿＿＿＿ ＿＿＿＿＿＿ ＿＿＿＿＿＿ by the teacher?

(4) そこで何が発見されましたか。　(find)

What ＿＿＿＿＿＿ ＿＿＿＿＿＿ there?

4 【表現】日本語に合う英文になるように，▢から適切な語を選んで空所に書きましょう。

(1) 新しい家はどんなですか。

＿＿＿＿＿＿ is your new house ＿＿＿＿＿＿?

(2) 日に日にクリスマスめいてきた。

It is getting more like Christmas ＿＿＿＿＿＿ ＿＿＿＿＿＿ ＿＿＿＿＿＿.

(3) 眠れますか。

＿＿＿＿＿＿ you ＿＿＿＿＿＿ ＿＿＿＿＿＿ sleep?

| to | day | like | what | day | are | able | by |

5 【内容理解】本文の内容に合うように，次の質問に対する適切な答えをア～エから選びましょう。

Why is the new type of airplane lighter?　　　　　　　　　　（　　　）

ア　Because it uses fewer materials.

イ　Because it has a lot of windows.

ウ　Because its walls and the ceiling are the speakers.

エ　Because the passengers can see the outside scenery on their laptop computer.

Yes. I'm on the baseball team called Applause.

29

1 【本文理解】音声を聞いて，区切りに気をつけて音読し，下の問いに答えましょう。

When we board an airplane, / flight attendants welcome us / with a smile. // We sometimes see ❶them / in their functional or traditional uniforms. // Their uniforms are also changing. // They ensure / our safety and comfort. //

The highlight of the flight / for us / is often the meal. // Most airlines offer / some sort of meal services / during flights. //
S   V   C
❷They may be / snacks and drinks / or an actual meal. // These are also changing. // When passengers can't eat / certain foods / because of their religion, / health, / or any other reason, / other food options / **G** can be provided. //

The airplane seats / are getting more comfortable / because ❸they are designed / on
（助動詞＋受動態）
the basis / of human engineering studies. //

The airplane is constantly evolving. //

Would you like to travel abroad / by airplane? //

(1) 下線部❶ them は誰を指すのか，文中の語句で答えましょう。　　　　　　　　＿＿＿＿＿

(2) 下線部❷ They 何を指すのか，文中の語句で答えましょう。　　　　　　　　　　＿＿＿＿＿

(3) 下線部❸ they は何を指すのか，文中の語句で答えなさい。　　　　　　　　　　＿＿＿＿＿

2 【単語】次の語句の意味を調べて書きましょう。

(1) attendant(s)　　名(　　　　　　　)　(2) functional　　形(　　　　　　　)
(3) traditional*　　形(　　　　　　　)　(4) ensure　　動(　　　　　　　)
(5) comfort　　名(　　　　　　　)　(6) highlight　　名(　　　　　　　)
(7) airline　　名(　　　　　　　)　(8) sort　　名(　　　　　　　)
(9) snack(s)　　名(　　　　　　　)　(10) religion　　名(　　　　　　　)
(11) option(s)　　名(　　　　　　　)　(12) on the basis of ～　　(　　　　　　　)
(13) engineering　　名(　　　　　　　)　(14) constantly　　副(　　　　　　　)

Nice Fit 本文から抜き出しましょう。

航空機に乗る ＝(　　　　　　　)(　　　　　　　)(　　　　　　　)

Coffee Break

functional（お尻につけて名詞から形容詞）
functional の -al のように，お尻につけて名詞から形容詞になるものに，下記のようなものがあります。
-al, -ous, -ic, -y, -ful, -able, -ive, -ible, -ish, -ly

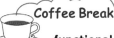

英会話 footwork

What kind of movies do you like to watch?

Grammar

助動詞＋受動態

〈助動詞＋be 動詞＋過去分詞〉で，受動態に助動詞の意味が加わります。

Other food options <u>can be provided</u>.
　　　　　　　　　　供給されうる

Bio-fuels, electricity, or solar energy <u>will be used by</u> new types of engines.
　　　　　　　　　　　　　　　　使用されるでしょう

受け身は語順にも注意が必要だよ。

助動詞を含む受動態は〈助動詞＋be＋過去分詞〉の形になるのよ。助動詞の後ろの動詞は原形だからね。

---

3 【文法】日本語に合う英文になるように，空所に適切な語を書きましょう。

(1) 今夜は満月が見られるよ。

A full moon ＿＿＿＿＿＿ ＿＿＿＿＿＿ ＿＿＿＿＿＿ tonight.

(2) 規則は守るべきだ。

The rule ＿＿＿＿＿＿ ＿＿＿＿＿＿ ＿＿＿＿＿＿.

(3) その約束は忘れてはならない。

The promise ＿＿＿＿＿＿ not ＿＿＿＿＿＿ ＿＿＿＿＿＿.

(4) コンサートは次の水曜日に開かれるだろう。

The concert ＿＿＿＿＿＿ ＿＿＿＿＿＿ ＿＿＿＿＿＿ next Wednesday.

---

4 【表現】日本語に合う英文になるように，□□□から適切な語を選んで空所に書きましょう。

(1) 美咲は顔に笑みをたたえて私にあいさつをした。

Misaki greeted me ＿＿＿＿＿＿ ＿＿＿＿＿＿ ＿＿＿＿＿＿ on her face.

(2) どんな種類の機内食が一番好きですか。

＿＿＿＿＿＿ ＿＿＿＿＿＿ ＿＿＿＿＿＿ in-flight meals do you like best?

(3) 雇用主は性別に基づく差別を行ってはいけないことになっている。

Employers are not allowed to discriminate ＿＿＿＿＿＿ ＿＿＿＿＿＿ ＿＿＿＿＿＿ of gender.

smile	a	with	of	kind	what	basis	the	on

---

5 【内容理解】本文の内容に合う文はＴを，合わない文はＦを〇で囲みましょう。

(1) Flight attendants' uniforms are not changing. （ T / F ）

(2) The highlight of the flight for us is often the movie. （ T / F ）

(3) When airline passengers can't eat certain foods, they have to skip them. （ T / F ）

(4) Airplanes are very often developing and changing. （ T / F ）

I like to watch comedies.

Lesson 4 Evolving Airplanes

まとめ

▶pp.48-61

1 【英語定義】次の英語の定義に相当する英単語を書きなさい。　〈5点×5〉
(1) move through the air as a bird does, using wings and engines　＿＿＿＿＿
(2) safe, not harmful to the environment, sustainable　＿＿＿＿＿
(3) style of dress worn by all members of an organization such as the police　＿＿＿＿＿
(4) top inner surface of a room, the highest limit　＿＿＿＿＿
(5) in a short time from now, early, quickly　＿＿＿＿＿

2 【ストーリー・リテリング】教科書 p.52(Section 1)を4回音読した後，次の語句をすべて用いて本文を自分の言葉で再現しなさい。　〈8点〉
　[使用語句]：the Wright brothers, 1903, first, history, carry

＿＿＿＿＿＿＿＿＿＿＿＿＿＿＿＿＿＿＿＿＿＿＿＿＿＿＿＿＿＿
＿＿＿＿＿＿＿＿＿＿＿＿＿＿＿＿＿＿＿＿＿＿＿＿＿＿＿＿＿＿
＿＿＿＿＿＿＿＿＿＿＿＿＿＿＿＿＿＿＿＿＿＿＿＿＿＿＿＿＿＿

3 【文法】次の各文を受動態を用いて書きかえなさい。　〈5点×4〉
(1) Who made this table?

＿＿＿＿＿＿＿＿＿＿＿＿＿＿＿＿＿＿＿＿＿＿＿＿＿＿＿＿＿＿?
(2) Mary will invite me to the prom.

＿＿＿＿＿＿＿＿＿＿＿＿＿＿＿＿＿＿＿＿＿＿＿＿＿＿＿＿＿＿.
(3) Saburo saw her sing at the stage.

＿＿＿＿＿＿＿＿＿＿＿＿＿＿＿＿＿＿＿＿＿＿＿＿＿＿＿＿＿＿.
(4) They paid no attention to her words.

＿＿＿＿＿＿＿＿＿＿＿＿＿＿＿＿＿＿＿＿＿＿＿＿＿＿＿＿＿＿.

4 【文法】日本語に合う英文になるように，（　）内の語を並べかえなさい。　〈5点×4〉
(1) 彼は流ちょうに英語が話せます。　(speak / fluently / English / can / he).

＿＿＿＿＿＿＿＿＿＿＿＿＿＿＿＿＿＿＿＿＿＿＿＿＿＿＿＿＿＿.
(2) ジョンはこの本を読んだはずがない。　John (have / book / can't / read / this).
　John ＿＿＿＿＿＿＿＿＿＿＿＿＿＿＿＿＿＿＿＿＿＿＿＿＿＿＿.
(3) この手紙はすぐに送られなければならない。　This letter (sent / once / be / at / must).
　This letter ＿＿＿＿＿＿＿＿＿＿＿＿＿＿＿＿＿＿＿＿＿＿＿＿.
(4) 会議は来週まで延期される予定です。　The meeting (put / will / till / week / off / next / be).
　The meeting ＿＿＿＿＿＿＿＿＿＿＿＿＿＿＿＿＿＿＿＿＿＿＿.

32

5 【内容理解】次の英文を読んで，下の問いに答えなさい。

〈計27点〉

Since ancient times, humans have been dreaming of flying in the sky. After various challenges, finally, the Wright brothers, Wilbur Wright and Orville Wright, ①(　　) fly a manned airplane on December 17th, 1903. Its name was Wright Flyer. It had a gasoline engine and two propellers. This was the ②very first flight in history. Orville Wright flew about 36.5 meters in 12 seconds. It was a great step for humankind. Since then, airplanes have developed greatly and evolved in various ways.

Now, an airplane ③(　　) fly more than ten thousand kilometers and carry more than five hundred people.

④What will airplanes be like in the future? One company is planning to invent a new type of airplane. The airplane will not have any windows. The walls and the ceiling will be the screens. The airplane has exterior cameras. The passengers can see the outside scenery on the screen. This type of airplane uses fewer materials, so it is lighter.

New types of engines will use bio-fuels, electricity, or solar energy. They will be eco-friendly and ⑤(　　) make much noise. ⑥(is / to / Mach 4.5 / be / the speed / expected), or 5,500 kilometers per hour. We will be able to enjoy a convenient and comfortable flight.

Airplanes are developing and evolving day by day.

What can you imagine future airplanes might look like?

(1) 下線部①，③，⑤がそれぞれ次の意味になるように，　　　から適切な助動詞を選んで書きなさい。

(3点×3)

① 「飛ばすことができた」　　　　　　　　　　　　　　　＿＿＿＿＿＿

③ 「飛ぶことができる」　　　　　　　　　　　　　　　　＿＿＿＿＿＿

⑤ 「それほど騒音を出さなくなるでしょう」　　　　　　　＿＿＿＿＿＿

| can | will | could | would | can't | won't |

(2) 下線部②の very と同じ用法のものを，次のア～エから選んで記号を書きなさい。　(3点)

ア　He talks very slowly.　　　　　　　　　　　　　　　　（　　　）

イ　Thank you very much.

ウ　She's very afraid of birds.

エ　That's the very airplane I saw yesterday.

(3) 下線部④を like の意味に注意して，日本語にしなさい。　(5点)

＿＿＿＿＿＿＿＿＿＿＿＿＿＿＿＿＿＿＿＿＿＿＿＿＿＿＿＿＿＿＿＿＿＿＿

(4) 下線部⑥が「マッハ4.5のスピードが期待されている」という意味になるように(　　)内の語句を並べかえなさい。　(5点)

＿＿＿＿＿＿＿＿＿＿＿＿＿＿＿＿＿＿＿＿＿＿＿＿＿＿＿＿＿＿＿＿＿＿＿

(5) 本文の内容に合うように，空所に入る語を書きなさい。　(5点)

ⓐ　The Wright brothers ＿＿＿＿＿ ＿＿＿＿＿ ＿＿＿＿＿ fly a manned airplane in 1903.

ⓑ　A new type of airplane uses ＿＿＿＿＿ ＿＿＿＿＿, so it is lighter.

1 【本文理解】音声を聞いて，区切りに気をつけて音読し，下の問いに答えましょう。

People / in fashionable clothes / appear on weekends / in a suburb of Brazzaville, /
  S   V

capital city / of Republic of Congo. // They are called "Sapeur." // It means / the Society /

for the Advancement / of Elegant People. //

Republic of Congo / is one of the poorest countries / in Africa. // The average income / is

about $300 / a month. // Sapeurs are not wealthy. // Nor are ❶they / fashion models. //
                                                    V   S   C

They are / just like everyone else / on weekdays. // They usually wear / casual clothes. //

However, / they buy / very expensive fashionable clothes. // These clothes / are much

more expensive / than their monthly salary. // They still enjoy / **G** wearing ❷them / only
                                                                （動名詞）

on weekends. //

(1) 下線部❶ they は誰を指すのか，文中の語で答えましょう。　　　　　　　＿＿＿＿＿＿

(2) 下線部❷ them は何を指すのか，文中の語句で答えましょう。　　　　　　＿＿＿＿＿＿

2 【単語】次の語句の意味を調べて書きましょう。

(1) fashionable　形（　　　　　　　）　(2) suburb　　　　名（　　　　　　　）

(3) republic　　　名（　　　　　　　）　(4) advancement　名（　　　　　　　）

(5) elegant　　　形（　　　　　　　）　(6) poor(est)　　 形（　　　　　　　）

(7) income　　　名（　　　　　　　）　(8) wealthy　　　形（　　　　　　　）

(9) nor　　　　　接（　　　　　　　）　(10) fashion　　　名（　　　　　　　）

(11) weekday(s)　名（　　　　　　　）　(12) casual　　　 形（　　　　　　　）

(13) monthly　　　形（　　　　　　　）　(14) salary　　　 名（　　　　　　　）

> **Coffee Break**
> 「動名詞だけを目的語とする動詞(句)」の主なものの頭文字を手がかりとして，
> **Daic Megafeps**(大工　メガフェップス)と覚えるのも１つの方法です。
> **D**(deny)　**a**(admit)　**i**(imagine)　**c**(consider)　**M**(mind, miss)　**e**(enjoy)　**g**(give up)
> **a**(avoid)　**f**(finish)　**e**(escape)　**p**(practice, put off,)　**s**(stop)

英会話 footwork

What do you like to talk about with your friends?

• Grammar

動名詞とは，進行形(現在分詞)と同形ですが，動詞と名詞の働きをかねそなえたものをいいます。

動名詞

動詞「～する」を -ing 形にして名詞「～すること」に変えます。

主語，目的語，補語，前置詞の目的語として使います。

動詞の -ing 形は名詞の働きをして，「～すること」という意味を表すんだね。

Wearing fashionable clothes is important for me. 主語

They still enjoy wearing them only on weekends. 目的語

動名詞は主語，目的語，補語や前置詞の目的語にもなるのよ。

My hobby is reading fashion magazines. 補語

I am fond of watching African movies. 前置詞の目的語

Nice Fit 本文から抜き出しましょう。 郊外に＝(　　　　　) (　　　　　) (　　　　　)

3 【文法】日本語に合う英文になるように，(　　)内の動詞を適切な形にかえて空所に書きましょう。

(1) 食べ過ぎることは健康によくない。 (eat)

_____ _____ _____ is not good for your health.

(2) 彼の趣味は山の写真を撮ることだった。 (take)

His hobby was _____ _____ _____ mountains.

(3) 私たちは遠来の客と話をして楽しんだ。 (talk)

We enjoyed _____ _____ the visitors from a distant place.

(4) 彼らはホラー小説を読むのが好きだ。 (read)

They are fond of _____ horror _____.

4 【表現】日本語に合う英文になるように，□□□から適切な語を選んで空所に書きましょう。

(1) 「行きたくないな」「私も」

"I don't want to go." "_____ _____ _____."

(2) 彼女は他の人よりはるかに仕事が丁寧だ。

She works _____ _____ _____ than the others.

| more | do | carefully | I | much | nor |

5 【内容理解】本文の内容に合う文はTを，合わない文はFを〇で囲みましょう。

(1) Sapeurs appear in fashionable clothes in a suburb of Brazzaville on weekends. (T / F)

(2) Republic of Congo is one of the richest countries in Africa. (T / F)

(3) Most Sapeurs are fashion models on weekdays. (T / F)

(4) Sapeurs wear clothes which are much more expensive than their monthly salary.

(T / F)

I like to talk about TV shows.

1 【本文理解】音声を聞いて，区切りに気をつけて音読し，下の問いに答えましょう。

> Republic of Congo / had been colonized / by France / from 1882 to 1960. // After ❶its
> S   V
>
> independence, / several civil wars occurred. // People / in Republic of Congo / wanted
>   S   V
>
> **G** to spend a peaceful life. // Sapeurs thought / that one way / **G** to make the country
> (不定詞)   (不定詞)
>
> peaceful / was by dressing up. // Violence makes / their expensive and beautiful clothes /
>
> dirty, / so they do not fight. // Their motto is / "Let's drop the weapons, / let us work / and
>   V   O   C
>
> dress elegantly." //
> C
>
> One Sapeur says, / "We should make sounds / in designer shoes, / not in military
>   S   V   O
>
> shoes." // Being a Sapeur / is not just about vanity. // Sapeurs dress nicely / and behave
>   S   V   C
>
> elegantly / for peace. // ❷They are respected / and admired / as a symbol of peace / in
>
> their communities. //

(1) 下線部❶ its は何を指すのか，文中の語句で答えましょう。　　　＿＿＿＿＿＿＿

(2) 下線部❷ They は誰を指すのか，文中の語で答えましょう。　　　　　＿＿＿＿＿＿＿

2 【単語】次の語句の意味を調べて書きましょう。

(1)	colonize(d)	動( )	(2)	independence	名( )
(3)	civil	形( )	(4)	occur(red)	動( )
(5)	violence	名( )	(6)	motto	名( )
(7)	weapon(s)	名( )	(8)	elegantly	副( )
(9)	designer	形( )	(10)	vanity	名( )
(11)	behave	動( )	(12)	admire(d)	動( )

Nice Fit 本文から抜き出しましょう。

数度にわたる内戦 = (   ) (   ) (   )

Coffee Break

independence（頭につけてつくる反意語）

independence の in- のように，頭につけて反意語をつくるものに，下記のようなものがあります。

im-, un-, mis-, dis-, non-

英会話
footwork

What do you do to relax?

● Grammar

不定詞とは，動詞の意味をもちながら，名詞・形容詞・副詞など
の働きをするものを指します。

不定詞①

〈to＋動詞の原形〉を不定詞といいます。

名詞的用法：「～すること」という意味になります。

形容詞的用法：「～するための，～すべき」という意味になります。

People in Republic of Congo wanted <u>to spend</u> a peaceful life.

I have a lot of work <u>to do</u> this week.

Sapeurs thought that one way <u>to make</u> the country peaceful was by dressing up.

語句のかたまりが
いろいろな品詞の
働きをするから「不
定詞」と言うのね。

ここでは，不定詞
が名詞，形容詞の
働きをしているん
だね。

3 【文法】日本語に合う英文になるように，(　　)内の語句を並べかえましょう。

(1) 英語をマスターすることは簡単ではない。　(English / not / to / easy / is / master).

_____.

(2) 彼は飛行機の中で読む本を何冊か買った。

He (to / some books / read / bought) in the airplane.

He _____ in the airplane.

(3) 私の仕事は皿とコップを洗うことだった。

(wash / to / was / job / my) the dishes and glasses.

_____ the dishes and glasses.

(4) 私たちを手伝ってくれる人を探している。　We are looking for (a man / help / us / to).

We are looking for _____.

4 【表現】日本語に合う英文になるように，□□□から適切な語を選んで空所に書きましょう。

(1) 食べたり飲んだりしようではないか，どうせあしたはあしたじゃないか。

_____ _____ eat and drink, for tomorrow is another day.

(2) キリマンジャロ山はアフリカのシンボルとして貴ばれている。

Mt. Kilimanjaro is admired _____ _____ _____ _____ Africa.

| us | let | symbol | as | a | of |

5 【内容理解】本文の内容に合うように，次の質問に対する適切な答えをア～エから選びましょう。

Why don't people called Sapeurs try to fight?　　　　　　　　　　　(　　　)

ア　Because they want to use many powerful weapons.

イ　Because violence makes their expensive and beautiful clothes dirty.

ウ　Because they like military shoes better than designer shoes.

エ　Because they are planning to colonize Republic of Congo.

I usually listen to jazz music.

1 【本文理解】音声を聞いて，区切りに気をつけて音読し，下の問いに答えましょう。

There are two Congos / in Africa. // One is / Republic of Congo. // The other is /
　　　　　　　　　　　　　　　　　　S　V　　　　　　　　　C

Democratic Republic of the Congo. // There are Sapeurs / in both countries. // However, /
　　　　　　　　　　　　　　　　　　　　　　V　　　　　S

they have / a different sense of fashion. // While Sapeurs in ❶the former country / like to

wear / colorful and formal suits, / those in ❷the latter / prefer black and unique outfits. //

G It is important / for both groups / to dress up, / so many of them / work hard /
(形式主語)

G to buy expensive clothes. //
　(不定詞)

　Although their fashions / are quite different, / their wish for peace / is the same. //
　　　　　　　　S'　　　　　　V'　　　　　C'　　　　　　　S　　　　　V　　C

Daniel Severin Mouyengo, / the chairman / of the Sapeur Association in Japan, / says, /

"We look out / for each other, / and no one is allowed / to fight. // In fact, / I would like the

Sapeur / to be effectively a vaccination / for peace." //

(1) 下線部❶ the former country とはどこの国を指すのか，文中の語句で答えましょう。＿＿＿＿＿＿

(2) 下線部❷ the latter とはどこの国を指すのか，文中の語句で答えましょう。＿＿＿＿＿＿

2 【単語】次の語句の意味を調べて書きましょう。

(1) republic* 名( ) (2) democratic 形( )

(3) while* 接( ) (4) former 形( )

(5) formal 形( ) (6) suit(s) 名( )

(7) latter 形( ) (8) outfit(s) 名( )

(9) although* 接( ) (10) chairman 名( )

(11) association 名( ) (12) vaccination 名( )

Nice Fit 平和のための予防接種＝( ) ( ) ( ) ( )

Coffee Break

vaccination(お尻につけて動詞から名詞)
vaccination の -tion のようにお尻につけて動詞から名詞にするときにつけるものに下記のようなものがあります。
-tion, -ment, -ance, -age, -al, -y

英会話 footwork

Where would you like to go on your next holiday?

Grammar

不定詞②

〈to＋動詞の原形〉を不定詞といいます。

副詞的用法：「～するために，～して」という意味になります。

副詞的用法の不定詞は，動詞・形容詞・副詞・文全体を修飾します。

They work hard <u>to buy</u> expensive clothes.

> 副詞の働きをする不定詞もあるんだ。

形式主語

〈It is＋形容詞＋(for 人)＋to＋動詞の原形〉の形で，「(人にとって)～することは(形容詞)だ」という意味を表します。

<u>It</u> is important <u>for</u> both groups <u>to</u> dress up.

(＝To dress up is important for both groups.)

> 英語では長い主語はバランスが悪く，好まれない。だから it という仮主語を置いて，本当の主語を後ろに持ってきて文の形をスッキリさせているのね。

3 【文法】(1)～(5)に続く最も適切なものをア～オから選んで(　)に書きましょう。

(1) We were shocked　　　(　　)　　　ア　to be a great scientist.

(2) The little baby grew up　　　(　　)　　　イ　enough to believe such a liar.

(3) My aunt went shopping　　　(　　)　　　ウ　to buy some food and drinks.

(4) It is easy　　　(　　)　　　エ　to hear the news.

(5) I was foolish　　　(　　)　　　オ　for him to read the book.

4 【表現】日本語に合う英文になるように，□□□から適切な語を選んで空所に書きましょう。

(1) 双子は別行動を取った。1人はタクシーに乗り，もう1人は歩いて家に帰った。

The twins went their separate ways. ＿＿＿＿＿＿ took a taxi, and ＿＿＿＿＿＿＿ ＿＿＿＿＿＿ walked home.

(2) お互いに気をつかうことが肝要だ。

It is very important ＿＿＿＿＿ ＿＿＿＿＿ ＿＿＿＿＿ ＿＿＿＿＿ ＿＿＿＿＿ other.

look	one	out	the	for	other	each	to

5 【内容理解】本文の内容に合うように，(　)内に適切な語を入れて要約を完成させましょう。

Republic of Congo is a very ①(　　　　　　) country in Africa. However, some people enjoy ②(　　　　　　) expensive fashionable clothes. They are called Sapeur. They don't fight because they don't want to ③(　　　　　　) their elegant clothes dirty. Many people respect them as a ④(　　　　　　) of peace. There are two Congos in Africa, and Sapeurs are in ⑤(　　　　　　) countries. Although their fashions are quite different, their ⑥(　　　　　　) for peace is the same. Daniel is the ⑦(　　　　　　) of the Sapeur Association in Japan.

> I'd like to go to Kyoto.

Lesson **5** The Symbol of Peace

まとめ

▶pp.62-73

1【英語定義】次の英語の定義に相当する英単語を書きなさい。　　　　　　　　　〈5点×5〉

(1) Saturday and Sunday as a period of rest or holiday　　　　　_____

(2) not clean, covered with dirt, (*informal*) unpleasant, dishonest, or mean　_____

(3) all the clothing or articles needed for a purpose　　　　　_____

(4) outlying residential district of a town or city　　　　　_____

(5) stand for　　　　　_____

2【ストーリー・リテリング】教科書 p.66（Section 2）を4回音読した後，次の語句をすべて用いて本文を自分の言葉で再現しなさい。　　　　　　　　　〈8点〉

[使用語句]：Congo,　France,　a peaceful life,　one way,　dressing up

_____

_____

_____

3【文法】日本語に合う英文になるように，（　　）内の語句を並べかえなさい。　　〈5点×4〉

(1) 彼女はひとりで富士山に登ることを決心した。　(she / Mt. Fuji / to / climb / decided / alone).

_____.

(2) 何か冷たい飲み物はいかがですか。　Would you like (cold / to / something / drink)?

Would you like _____?

(3) 教子は成長して教師になった。　Kyoko (be / grew / teacher / to / a / up).

Kyoko _____.

(4) 彼がその問題を解くのは簡単だ。　(is / solve / easy / it / him / for / to) the problem.

_____ the problem.

4【文法】日本語に合う英文になるように，空所に適切な語を書きなさい。　　〈5点×4〉

(1) 智恵理は私が部屋入っていくとギターをひくのをやめた。

Chieri stopped _____ _____ _____ when I entered the room.

(2) ハロルドはその雑誌を読み終わったのですか。

Has Harold _____ _____ the magazine?

(3) 間違いをすることを恐れてはならない。

Don't _____ _____ _____ _____ mistakes.

(4) 私の父はテレビでラグビーを見て楽しんだ。

My father _____ _____ rugby _____ _____.

5 【内容理解】次の英文を読んで，下の問いに答えなさい。　　　　　　　　　　　〈計27点〉

　　People in fashionable clothes appear on weekends in a suburb of Brazzaville, capital city of Republic of Congo. They are ①(call) "Sapeur." It means the Society for the Advancement of Elegant People.

　　Republic of Congo is one of the poorest ②(country) in Africa. The average income is about $300 a month. Sapeurs are not wealthy. ③Nor are they fashion models. They are just like everyone else on weekdays. They usually wear casual clothes. However, they buy very expensive fashionable clothes. These clothes are much more expensive than their monthly salary. They still enjoy ④(wear) them only on weekends.

　　Republic of Congo had been colonized by France from 1882 to 1960. After its independence, several civil wars occurred. People in Republic of Congo wanted ⑤(spend) a peaceful life. Sapeurs thought that one way ⑥to make the country peaceful was by ⑦(dress) up. Violence makes their expensive and beautiful clothes dirty, so they do not fight. Their motto is "Let's drop the weapons, let us work and dress elegantly."

　　One Sapeur says, "⑧We should make sounds in designer shoes, not in military shoes." Being a Sapeur is not just about vanity. Sapeurs dress nicely and behave elegantly for peace. They are respected and admired as a symbol of peace in their communities.

(1) 次のそれぞれの英語による定義に相当する英単語を本文中から抜き出しなさい。　　(2点×3)

　　ⓐ outside community of a town or city　　　　　　　　　_____

　　ⓑ careless and informal　　　　　　　　　　　　　　　_____

　　ⓒ short sentence or phrase as a guide or rule of behavior　_____

(2) ①，②，④，⑤，⑦の（　　）内の語を適切な形に直して書きなさい。　　(2点×5)

　　① _____　② _____　④ _____　⑤ _____　⑦ _____

(3) 下線部③とほぼ同じ意味になるように，次の空所に適切な語を書きなさい。　　(2点)

　　Sapeurs are not fashion models, _____.

(4) 下線部⑥の不定詞と同じ用法のものをア〜エから１つ選び，記号で答えなさい。　(2点)

　　ア　To learn English is rather difficult.　　　　　　　　　（　　　）

　　イ　He has made a promise to come at ten.

　　ウ　The water in this small river is good to drink.

　　エ　I am awfully sorry to trouble you so much.

(5) 下線部⑧を日本語にしなさい。　　(4点)

　　_____

(6) 本文の内容に合う文はTを，合わない文はFを○で囲みなさい。　　(3点)

　　ⓐ Brasilia is the capital city of Republic of Congo.　　　　　　　　（ T / F ）

　　ⓑ Sapeurs are wealthy enough to buy very expensive fashionable clothes.　（ T / F ）

　　ⓒ Sapeurs dress nicely and behave elegantly to make their own country peaceful.（ T / F ）

Lesson 6 Serendipity

1 【本文理解】音声を聞いて，区切りに気をつけて音読し，下の問いに答えましょう。

Have you ever heard / the word / "serendipity"? // It means / making valuable discoveries / by accident. //

In 1853, / a shrewish guest / came to a restaurant / in New York. // He was Cornelius Vanderbilt, / an American millionaire. // He ordered French fries, / and when he saw them, / he said, / "These are / too thick to eat!" // He sent them back / again and again. // George Crum, / the chef **G** cooking in the kitchen, / got really angry. // **❶**He cut the
（分詞の後置修飾）
potatoes / extremely thin, / just like pieces of paper. // **❷**They curled / and became crisp. // "Take that! // He can't stab them / with a fork." // However, / Vanderbilt said, / "How delicious!" // They became a popular item / on the menu / at the restaurant. //
S   V   C
In this way, / the first potato chips / are said to originate / from a chef's anger. //

(1) 下線部❶ He は誰を指すのか，文中の語句で答えましょう。　　＿＿＿＿＿

(2) 下線部❷ They は何を指すのか，文中の語句で答えましょう。　　＿＿＿＿＿

2 【単語】次の語句の意味を調べて書きましょう。

(1)	serendipity	名( )	(2)	valuable*	形( )	
(3)	shrewish	形( )	(4)	millionaire	名( )	
(5)	chef	名( )	(6)	cook(ing)	動( )	
(7)	extremely	副( )	(8)	curl(ed)	動( )	
(9)	crisp	形( )	(10)	stab	動( )	
(11)	fork	名( )	(12)	chip(s)	名( )	
(13)	originate	動( )	(14)	anger	名( )	

Nice Fit 本文から抜き出しましょう。激怒した ＝( )( )( )

☕ **Coffee Break**

shrewish（お尻につけて名詞から形容詞）
shrewish の -ish のように，お尻につけて名詞から形容詞にするものに，下記のようなものがあります。
-ish, -al, -ous, -ic, -y, -ful, -able, -ive, -ible, -ly

英会話 footwork

Do you think that, in the future, more people will take cooking lessons in their free time?

分詞の後置修飾

2種類の分詞　現在分詞（動詞の ing 形）・過去分詞（規則／不規則変化）

現在分詞：名詞の後に現在分詞を置き「～している…」と名詞を修飾することができます。

過去分詞：名詞の後に過去分詞を置き「～される…」と名詞を修飾することができます。

分詞一語で名詞を修飾するときは，名詞の前に分詞を置きます。（一語だけなら名詞の前に，二語以上なら名詞の後にくる分詞）

George Crum, the **chef** cooking in the kitchen, got really angry.

The thin **potatoes** fried by the chef were delicious.

後置修飾は，日本語ではめったに用いられない表現手段なので，特に注意が必要だね。

現在分詞には「している」という進行形の意味が，過去分詞には「される，された」という受け身の意味があるのよ。

3 【文法】日本語に合う英文になるように，(　　　)内の語句を並べかえましょう。

(1) この眠っている赤ちゃんをごらんなさい。　Look (sleeping / at / baby / this).

Look _____.

(2) 池で泳いでいる魚をつかまえてください。

Please catch the (the pond / swimming / in / fish).

Please catch the _____.

(3) 興奮している観客が立ち上がって絶叫した。(audience / excited / the) stood up and shouted.

_____ stood up and shouted.

(4) 愛は旅行中にとった写真を私に見せた。Ai showed me (during / taken / some photos / the tour).

Ai showed me _____.

4 【表現】日本語に合う英文になるように，☐☐☐から適切な語を選んで空所に書きましょう。

(1) 彼らに公園で会ったのはまったくの偶然だった。

We met them in the park quite _____ _____.

(2) これらの楽器は韓国の伝統文化に由来すると言われている。

These musical instruments are said to _____ _____ traditional Korean culture.

from	by	originate	accident

5 【内容理解】本文の内容に合う文はTを，合わない文はFを○で囲みましょう。

(1) "Serendipity" means making valuable discoveries as expected.　　(T / F)

(2) Cornelius Vanderbilt was not satisfied with the French fries served to him first. (T / F)

(3) George Crum, the chef, got angry and threw a shrewish guest out of the restaurant.

(T / F)

(4) The first potato chips are said to have been born at a restaurant in New York. (T / F)

Yes. They want to learn how to cook new types of dishes.

Lesson 6 Serendipity

1 【本文理解】音声を聞いて，区切りに気をつけて音読し，下の問いに答えましょう。

In 1969, / Spencer Silver, / an American chemist, / tried to invent / a strong glue, / but he happened to invent / a strange glue. // It stuck easily, / but was easily removed. // It was a complete misfire. // When he looked at the glue / under a microscope, / however, / he became interested / in it. // Then he said to Art Fry, / his colleague, / "Do you think / this strange glue / might be useful?" // He answered, / "❶It peels / so easily. // Who wants / such a glue?" //

Five years later, / an idea came to Art's mind / when he <kbd>G</kbd> saw a bookmark / falling (知覚動詞) from his book. // ❷He said to himself, / "Wow! // This bookmark / can stay put / between pages / when we use that weak glue!" // In this way, / sticky notes / were first created. //

(1) 下線部❶ It は何を指すのか，文中の語句で答えましょう。＿＿＿＿＿＿

(2) 下線部❷ He は誰を指すのか，文中の語句で答えましょう。＿＿＿＿＿＿

2 【単語】次の語句の意味を調べて書きましょう。

(1) chemist　　　名(　　　　　)　(2) glue　　　　　名(　　　　　)

(3) stick > stuck*　動(　　　　　)　(4) easily*　　　副(　　　　　)

(5) misfire　　　名(　　　　　)　(6) microscope　名(　　　　　)

(7) colleague　　名(　　　　　)　(8) peel(s)　　　動(　　　　　)

(9) Who wants ～?*　(　　　　　)　(10) bookmark　　名(　　　　　)

(11) wow　　　　間(　　　　　)　(12) sticky　　　形(　　　　　)

Nice Fit 本文から抜き出しましょう。

付箋が産声をあげた＝(　　　　　) (　　　　　) (　　　　　) (　　　　　) (　　　　　)

Coffee Break

misfire（頭につけてつくる反意語）
misfire の mis- のように，頭につけて反意語をつくるものに，下記のようなものがあります。
mis-, un-, in-(im-), dis-, non-

英会話 footwork

Do you think schools should have more sports events for their students?

• Grammar

知覚動詞

see / hear / feel など，「感覚」を表す「見る・聞く・感じる」動詞を知覚動詞と言います。
S＋V（知覚動詞）＋O＋動詞の原形（原形不定詞）：「O が〜するのを V する」
S＋V（知覚動詞）＋O＋動詞の ing 形（現在分詞）：「O が〜しているのを V する」
People <u>felt</u> the strange glue <u>peel</u> so easily.
An idea came to Art's mind when he <u>saw</u> a bookmark <u>falling</u> from his book.

C に動詞の原形が入ると，O が行う動作の一部始終（動作の始めから終わりまで）を表すのね。C に分詞が入ると，「O が C している［される］のを〜する」という意味を表します。

「知覚動詞」というのは，see，hear，feel などの感覚を表す動詞のことだよ。「親分，テーヘンダー！」のように自分が見聞きしてきた出来事を報告する際に威力を発揮しますね。

3　【文法】日本語に合う英文になるように，（　　）内の語句を並べかえましょう。

(1)　少年が背後から私の名前を呼ぶのが聞こえた。

I (the boy / my name / call / heard) from behind.

I ＿＿＿＿＿＿＿＿＿＿＿＿＿＿＿＿＿＿＿＿＿＿ from behind.

(2)　君はその男が部屋に入るのを見たのかね。　Did you (the man / see / the room / enter)?

Did you ＿＿＿＿＿＿＿＿＿＿＿＿＿＿＿＿＿＿＿＿＿？

(3)　彼女は暗闇の中で何かが動くのを聞いた。　She (move / heard / in / something) the dark.

She ＿＿＿＿＿＿＿＿＿＿＿＿＿＿＿＿＿＿＿ the dark.

(4)　私は自分の興味がどんどんわいてきているのを感じた。　(felt / rising / interest / my / I).

＿＿＿＿＿＿＿＿＿＿＿＿＿＿＿＿＿＿＿＿＿＿＿＿．

4　【表現】日本語に合う英文になるように，▭から適切な語を選んで空所に書きましょう。

(1)　もしかして吉川真教授をご存知ですか。

Do you ＿＿＿＿＿ ＿＿＿＿＿ ＿＿＿＿＿ Prof. Makoto Yoshikawa?

(2)　ミッション・マネージャーたちは「ハヤブサ２よ，ありがとう！」と心の中で思った。

The mission managers ＿＿＿＿＿ ＿＿＿＿＿ ＿＿＿＿＿, "Thank you, Hayabusa 2!"

themselves	to	said	know	happen	to

5　【内容理解】本文の内容に合うように，次の質問に対する適切な答えをア〜エから選びましょう。

When were sticky notes or Post-its first created?　　　　　　　　（　　）

ア　They were created in America in 1969.

イ　It was when Spencer Silver became a chemist in 1964.

ウ　It was in 1974 when Spencer Silver saw a bookmark falling from his book.

エ　They were created by Art Fry in 1974.

No. Students should have more time for studying.

Lesson 6 Serendipity

Lesson 6 Serendipity

Lesson 6 Serendipity

1 【本文理解】音声を聞いて，区切りに気をつけて音読し，下の問いに答えましょう。

> In 1904, / the Louisiana Purchase Exposition / was held / in Missouri, / the U.S.A. // It was so hot a day / that there was a long line / at the ice-cream stand. // The ice-cream seller said, / "I'm running out of paper dishes / for these ice creams!" // Next to him, / the other seller, / Ernest Hamwi, / sold zalabia, / a waffle-like pastry. // ❶He said, "Hey, bro! // Use these pastries / as substitutes / for paper dishes." // "Good idea!" / said the ice-cream seller. // Then ❷he [G] had Hamwi / roll the zalabia / into a cone shape / to hold the ice cream. // This zalabia cone / is believed to be / the origin / of the current / ice-cream cone. // Great inventions / often came / by mistake / or by chance. // Such serendipities / might also happen / around you. //
>
> （使役動詞）
> S　　V　　　　C

(1) 下線部❶ He は誰を指すのか，文中の語句で答えましょう。　——————

(2) 下線部❷ he は誰を指すのか，文中の語句で答えましょう。　——————

2 【単語】次の語句の意味を調べて書きましょう。

(1) purchase 名( ) (2) exposition 名( )

(3) Missouri 名( ) (4) seller 名( )

(5) ice-cream 形( ) (6) run out of ～* ( )

(7) zalabia 名( ) (8) waffle 名( )

(9) pastry 名( ) (10) hey 間( )

(11) bro 名( ) (12) substitute(s) 名( )

(13) cone 名( ) (14) current 形( )

Nice Fit 本文から抜き出しましょう。

今日のアイスクリームコーン＝( ) ( ) ( ) ( )

Coffee Break

I scream, "Ice cream!"（英語ごろ合わせ）

「アイスクリーム！」と私は甲高い声で叫ぶ。クリームの冷たいのを愛すから「愛すクリーム」としゃれてみたり，非情な冷たい「高利貸し」を ice-man などと和製英語を使うのは「高利」と「氷」とをかけた効率のよいしゃれですね。

英会話 footwork

Do you feel more Japanese people will travel to foreign countries in the future?

• Grammar

使役動詞

「(誰かに)～させる」という意味の動詞を使役動詞と言います。

S＋V(使役動詞)＋O＋原形不定詞(動詞の原形)：「O に～させる」

使役動詞には，have，make のほか let などがあります。

Then he <u>had</u> Hamwi <u>roll</u> the zalabia into a cone shape to hold the ice cream.

My father <u>made</u> me <u>wait</u> outside the ice-cream shop.

使役動詞(make, have, let など)の目的格補語には動詞の原形を用いるということね。

ただし，使役動詞として使われる get のみ，〈get＋人＋to ～〉を使うんだよ。

---

3 【文法】日本語に合う英文になるように，(　　)内の語句を並べかえましょう。

(1) 祖母はときどき私を買い物に行かせる。

Grandmother sometimes (shopping / me / makes / go).

Grandmother sometimes ＿＿＿＿＿＿＿＿＿＿＿＿＿＿＿＿＿＿＿＿＿＿＿.

(2) 先生は一人の生徒にその歌を歌わせた。　The teacher (the song / made / sing / one student).

The teacher ＿＿＿＿＿＿＿＿＿＿＿＿＿＿＿＿＿＿＿＿＿＿＿.

(3) 彼女は秘書に郵便物を送らせた。　She (the mail / had / send / the secretary).

She ＿＿＿＿＿＿＿＿＿＿＿＿＿＿＿＿＿＿＿＿＿＿＿.

(4) 自己紹介させていただきます。　Please (myself / introduce / me / let).

Please ＿＿＿＿＿＿＿＿＿＿＿＿＿＿＿＿＿＿＿＿＿＿＿.

4 【表現】日本語に合う英文になるように，□□□から適切な語を選んで空所に書きましょう。

(1) 食糧がなくなりかけている。

We ＿＿＿＿＿＿ ＿＿＿＿＿＿ ＿＿＿＿＿＿ ＿＿＿＿＿＿ food.

(2) 彼女はうっかりしてパスポートを家に忘れた。

She left her passport at home ＿＿＿＿＿＿ ＿＿＿＿＿＿.

| of | by | out | are | running | mistake |

5 【内容理解】本文の内容に合う文はTを，合わない文はFを○で囲みましょう。

(1) The Missouri Purchase Exposition was held in Louisiana, the U.S.A. in 1904. （T / F）

(2) It was such a hot day that there was a long line at the ice-cream stand. （T / F）

(3) The ice-cream seller was running out of paper dishes for the ice creams. （T / F）

(4) The ice-cream seller rolled the zalabia into a cone shape to hold the ice cream. （T / F）

Yes. There are many exciting things to see in foreign countries.

1 【英語定義】次の英語の定義に相当する英単語を書きなさい。 〈5点×5〉

(1) talent for making fortunate and unexpected discoveries by chance _____

(2) something placed between the pages of a book to mark the place _____

(3) person or thing taking the place of, acting for or serving for another _____

(4) head cook in a hotel or restaurant _____

(5) come across _____

2 【ストーリー・リテリング】教科書 p.76（Section 1）を4回音読した後，次の語句をすべて用いて本文を自分の言葉で再現しなさい。 〈10点〉

［使用語句］：1853, French fries, the chef, thin, potato chips

_____

_____

_____

3 【文法】日本語に合う英文になるように，（　　）内の語を並べかえなさい。 〈5点×4〉

(1) あの眠っている犬の名前は何ですか。　What's the name (that / dog / sleeping / of)?

What's the name _____?

(2) この壊れた椅子をごらんなさい。　Look (chair / broken / this / at).

Look _____.

(3) あそこで走っている男性をご存じですか。

Do (the / running / man / know / over there / you)?

Do _____?

(4) ブラジルで話されている言葉は何ですか。　(is / the / spoken / language / Brazil / what / in)?

_____?

4 【文法】日本語に合う英文になるように，適切な語を空所に書きなさい。 〈6点×3〉

(1) 父は私に車を洗わせた。

My father _____ _____ _____ the car.

(2) 私は彼女が博物館に入って行くのを見た。

I _____ _____ _____ into the museum.

(3) 私はその時だれかが私に触っているなあと感じた。

I _____ _____ _____ me then.

5 【内容理解】次の英文を読んで，下の問いに答えなさい。 〈計27点〉

Have you ever heard the word, "serendipity"? It means ①(discoveries, by, valuable, accident, making).

In 1853, a shrewish guest came to a restaurant in New York. He was Cornelius Vanderbilt, an American millionaire. He ordered French fries, and when he saw them, he said, "These are ②(　　) thick to eat!" He sent them back again and again. George Crum, ③厨房で調理中の料理長, got really angry. He cut the potatoes extremely ④(　　), just like pieces of paper. They curled and became crisp. "Take that! He can't stab them ⑤(　　) a fork." However, Vanderbilt said, "How delicious!" They became a popular item on the menu at the restaurant.

In this way, the first potato chips are said to originate from a chef's anger.

In 1969, Spencer Silver, an American chemist, tried to invent a strong glue, but he happened to invent a strange glue. It stuck easily, but was easily removed. It was a complete misfire. When he looked at the glue under a microscope, however, he became interested ⑥(　　) it. Then he said to Art Fry, his colleague, "Do you think this strange glue might be useful?" He answered, "It peels so easily. Who wants such a glue?"

⑦Five years later, an idea came to Art's mind when he saw a bookmark falling from his book. He said to himself, "Wow! This bookmark can stay put between pages when we use that weak glue!" In this way, ⑧ [　　　　　　　　] were first created.

(1) ①の(　　)内の語を並べかえて，serendipity の定義となるようにしなさい。 (3点)

serendipity ≒ (　　　　　　　　　　　　　　　　　　　　　　　　　　　)

(2) 文脈から考えて，②，④，⑤，⑥の空所に入る最も適切な語を書きなさい。 (2点×4)

②＿＿＿＿＿　④＿＿＿＿＿　⑤＿＿＿＿＿　⑥＿＿＿＿＿

(3) ③の意味を表す英語表現として次のうちどれが適切か，記号で答えなさい。 (3点)

ア cooking in the kitchen the chef 　　　　　　　　　　　　(　　)

イ in the kitchen cooking the chef

ウ the chef cooking in the kitchen

(4) 下線部⑦を日本語にしなさい。 (7点)

_____

(5) ⑧の空所に入れるのに最も適切な語句をア〜エから1つ選び，記号で答えなさい。 (2点)

ア staplers 　　　　　　　　　　　　　　　　　　　　　　(　　)

イ Ziploc bags

ウ sticky notes

エ masking tapes

(6) 本文の内容に合うように，次の質問に対する適切な答えを完成させなさい。 (4点)

From what are the first potato chips said to originate?

── They say that the first potato chips originate from a ＿＿＿＿＿ ＿＿＿＿＿.

7 The Secrets Hidden in Vermeer's Works

1 【本文理解】音声を聞いて，区切りに気をつけて音読し，下の問いに答えましょう。

In 1632, / one of the most popular artists / was born / in Delft, / the Netherlands. // His
　　　　　　　　　S　　　　　　　　　　　　　　V
name was Johannes Vermeer. // His famous works / have been exhibited / at museums in

Japan / many times. // Therefore, / there are many Japanese / **G** who are big fans / of
　　　　　　　　　　　　　　　　　　　V　　　　　　S　　　　　　　　　　　S′　　　V′　　　　　C′
　　　　　　　　　　　　　　　　　　　　　　　　　　　　　　　　　　　　　（主格の関係代名詞）
his works. // While his name is well known / all over the world, / his paintings / are full of

mysteries. // Until ❶he passed away / at the age of 43, / it is said / that he had created /

only 50 to 60 paintings, / and 35 pieces of them / are left today. // In spite of the small

number / of his works, / almost all of them / are said to be / masterpieces. //

　❷They have traveled / all over the world / for exhibition. // They have been stolen / at

least five times / so far. // Why are people so fascinated / with his works? // Let's find /

some attractive points / in his paintings. //

(1) 下線部❶ he は誰を指すのか，文中の語句で答えましょう。　　　　　　　　＿＿＿＿＿＿

(2) 下線部❷ They は何を指すのか，文中の語句で答えましょう。　　　　　　＿＿＿＿＿＿

2 【単語】次の語句の意味を調べて書きましょう。

(1)	exhibit(ed)	動( )	(2)	therefore*	副(	)
(3)	museum*	名( )	(4)	mystery*	名(	)
(5)	away	副( )	(6)	at the age of ~*	(	)
(7)	in spite of ~	( )	(8)	masterpiece(s)	名(	)
(9)	exhibition*	名( )	(10)	at least*	副(	)
(11)	fascinate(d)	動( )	(12)	attractive	形(	)

Nice Fit 本文から抜き出しましょう。

世界中いたる所で ＝(　　　) (　　　) (　　　) (　　　)

Coffee Break

exhibit 「頭がエキスパーとで外に出る，出す」
こんな覚え方はどうですか？　ex-, ec-, es-, super-, sur- が頭につくと，「外に出る，出す」のような意味
になるので。

英会話
footwork　　　　　　　Do you think people will spend more money on cell phones in the future?

• Grammar

関係代名詞（主格）

名詞句を後ろから修飾し，その文の主語としての働きをします。

who：先行詞（修飾される名詞句）が「人」の場合に用います。

which：先行詞（修飾される名詞句）が「人以外」の場合に用います。

先行詞の種類にかかわらず，that を主格の関係代名詞として用いることもできます。

There are many <u>Japanese</u> (who are big fans of his works).

This is a <u>map</u> (which shows the way to the museum).

who は先行詞が「人」の場合に，which は先行詞が「物」や「動物」の場合に使う。

that は先行詞が「人」でも「物」でも「動物」でも使えるのよ。

3 【文法】日本語に合う英文になるように，（　　）内の関係代名詞を用いて空所に書きましょう。

(1) 私はアラビア語を上手に話せるその女の子を知っている。　(who)

I know ＿＿＿＿＿ ＿＿＿＿＿ ＿＿＿＿＿ ＿＿＿＿＿ ＿＿＿＿＿ Arabic well.

(2) これはドイツ製のオープンカーだ。　(which)

This is the convertible ＿＿＿＿＿ ＿＿＿＿＿ ＿＿＿＿＿ ＿＿＿＿＿ Germany.

(3) 私は助けてくれたその男性に感謝した。　(who)

I thanked ＿＿＿＿＿ ＿＿＿＿＿ ＿＿＿＿＿ ＿＿＿＿＿ ＿＿＿＿＿.

(4) ハワイはカカオ豆を産するアメリカで唯一の州だ。　(that)　(注) produce cacao beans

Hawaii is the only state ＿＿＿＿＿ ＿＿＿＿＿ ＿＿＿＿＿ ＿＿＿＿＿ in the United
States.

4 【表現】日本語に合う英文になるように，□□□から適切な語を選んで書きましょう。

(1) ケンは昨年亡くなった。　Ken ＿＿＿＿＿ ＿＿＿＿＿ last year.

(2) 私は今までに少なくとも 6 回渡仏したことがある。

I have been to France ＿＿＿＿＿ ＿＿＿＿＿ six times ＿＿＿＿＿ ＿＿＿＿＿.

(3) 私はそのリズムに引き込まれた。　I was ＿＿＿＿＿ ＿＿＿＿＿ the rhythm.

| away | least | far | fascinated | at | passed | with | so |

5 【内容理解】本文の内容に合う文は T を，合わない文は F を○で囲みましょう。

(1) The great artist, Johannes Vermeer, was born in Amsterdam, the Netherlands in 1632.

(T / F)

(2) Vermeer's works have been exhibited at museums in Japan over and over again. (T / F)

(3) Although Vermeer created 50 to 60 paintings, most of them are said to be poor works.

(T / F)

(4) One of the most popular artists, Vermeer, passed away when he was 43 years old.

(T / F)

Yes. New models are becoming more expensive.

1 【本文理解】音声を聞いて，区切りに気をつけて音読し，下の問いに答えましょう。

Vermeer's nickname is / "the magician of light." // Look at "Milkmaid," / one of his most important works. // You can see / the light from the window / create soft shadow / in the
S   V   O   C
woman's face, / hands, / and clothing. // Like this painting, / there is often a window / on the left side / of his works. // In this way, / he mastered / how to change / our perception of figures / with light. //

Another characteristic / is the use of color. // Look at his most well-known work, / "Girl with a Pearl Earring." // The blue cloth / **G** which the girl wears / on her head / is a
S   (目的格の関係代名詞) S'   V   V
Turkish turban. // It shows / that Turkish culture / influenced / art in Europe / in the 17th
C   S V   S'   V'   O'
century. // Vermeer used the color / called "Vermeer blue" / to paint the turban. // ❶It was made / from lapis lazuli, / a deep-blue mineral. // In those days, / ❷it was almost as expensive / as pure gold. // Nevertheless, / he used it abundantly / for his paintings. //

(1)　下線部❶ It は何を指すのか，文中の語句で答えましょう。　　　　　　　　＿＿＿＿＿＿

(2)　下線部❷ it は何を指すのか，文中の語句で答えましょう。　　　　　　　　＿＿＿＿＿＿

2 【単語】次の語句の意味を調べて書きましょう。

(1) magician　名(　　　　　　　)　(2) Milkmaid　名(　　　　　　　)

(3) shadow　名(　　　　　　　)　(4) clothing　名(　　　　　　　)

(5) master(ed)　動(　　　　　　　)　(6) perception　名(　　　　　　　)

(7) figure　名(　　　　　　　)　(8) characteristic　名(　　　　　　　)

(9) pearl　名(　　　　　　　)　(10) earring　名(　　　　　　　)

(11) Turkish　形(　　　　　　　)　(12) turban　名(　　　　　　　)

(13) lapis lazuli　名(　　　　　　　)　(14) mineral　名(　　　　　　　)

(15) pure　形(　　　　　　　)　(16) nevertheless　副(　　　　　　　)

(17) abundantly　副(　　　　　　　)

Nice Fit 本文から抜き出しましょう。その当時は =(　　　　　)(　　　　　)(　　　　　)

Do you guess that there will be more TV programs about animals in the future?

Grammar

関係代名詞（目的格）

名詞句を後ろから修飾し，その文の目的語としての働きをします。
who(m)：先行詞が「人」の場合に用います（who(m)は省略可能）。
which：先行詞が「人以外」の場合に用います（which は省略可能）。
先行詞の種類にかかわらず，that を目的格の関係代名詞として用いることもできます。

Vermeer is **an excellent artist** (who(m) people all over the world love).

The blue cloth (which the girl wears on her head) is a Turkish turban.

目的格の関係代名詞 は that も which も who, whom もみんな 省略できるよ。

whom は who の目的格の形。話し言葉ではふつう who が使われるんだ。

3 【文法】日本語に合う英文になるように，（　　）内の語句を並べかえましょう。

(1) これは私があなたに紹介したい女性です。

This is (to you / the lady / introduce / want to / I / whom).

This is _____.

(2) あれは父が昨日買ったパターだ。　　That is (yesterday / the putter / that / my father / bought).

That is _____.

(3) 先週なくした帽子は見つかったかい。

Have you found (which / last week / lost / the cap / you)?

Have you found _____?

(4) これが私が今持っている全額のお金だ。　　This is (that / I / now / have / money / all the).

This is _____.

4 【表現】日本語に合う英文になるように，□□□から適切な語を選んで空所に書きましょう。

(1) このようにして，インターネットはコミュニケーションの方法に大変革をもたらした。

_____ _____ _____, the Internet has revolutionized the way we communicate.

(2) あの油絵の具はムール貝からつくられている。

That oil paint _____ _____ _____ blue mussel.

| from | made | is | way | this | in |

5 【内容理解】本文の内容に合うように，次の質問に対する適切な答えをア～エから選びましょう。

What does the blue cloth which the "Girl with a Pearl Earring" wears on her head show?

（　　）

ア　It shows that Vermeer regularly wore a Turkish turban, when painting.

イ　It shows that Vermeer's nickname is "the magician of light."

ウ　It shows that Turkish culture influenced art in Europe in the 17th century.

エ　It shows that lapis lazuli, a deep-blue mineral, was almost as expensive as natural pearls.

Yes. They want to learn more about different kinds of animals.

1 【本文理解】音声を聞いて，区切りに気をつけて音読し，下の問いに答えましょう。

In contrast with his reputation today, / Vermeer didn't necessarily succeed / as a
                                              S   V
painter / in life. // He had eleven children, / and they had ❶<u>a lot of</u> debt. // One of his
                                                                                            S
works / was on a wall / in a bakery. // It is said / that he handed over his works / to pay
   V
for the bread. // In fact, / he sold many of his works / very cheaply / to earn a living. //
Even about 200 years after his death, / "Girl with a Pearl Earring" / was sold / for only
two guilders and 30 cents. // Many of his works / gradually became valuable / long after
he died. // Today, / ❷it is quite a famous painting / **G** whose value is priceless. //
                        S V   C   (所有格の関係代名詞) S´ V´ C´
   Salvador Dali, / a Spanish artist, said, / "Vermeer had / the enthusiasm and distress /
to make / what is already perfect / even more perfect." // Why don't you see / his
masterpieces / first-hand? //

(1) 下線部❶a lot of を他の英語1語で答えましょう。　　　　　　　　　　＿＿＿＿＿＿＿

(2) 下線部❷it は何を指すのか，文中の固有名詞(5語)で答えましょう。　＿＿＿＿＿＿＿＿＿＿＿

2 【単語】次の語句の意味を調べて書きましょう。

(1) in contrast with ～　　　（　　　　　　　　）
(2) reputation　　名（　　　　　　　　）
(3) necessarily　副（　　　　　　　　）
(4) debt　　名（　　　　　　　　）
(5) bakery　　名（　　　　　　　　）
(6) hand over ～*　　（　　　　　　　　）
(7) in fact*　　（　　　　　　　　）
(8) cheaply　副（　　　　　　　　）
(9) guilder(s)　名（　　　　　　　　）
(10) priceless　形（　　　　　　　　）
(11) enthusiasm　名（　　　　　　　　）
(12) distress　名（　　　　　　　　）

 Nice Fit 本文から抜き出しましょう。

彼の傑作を自分の目で見る = (　　　　　)(　　　　　)(　　　　　)(　　　　　)

Coffee Break

ダリ (1904～1989)　シュールレアリズム (**surrealism**)！　「頭がエキスパートで外に出る。」
こんな覚え方はどうですか？　sur-, ex-, ec-, es-, super- が頭につくと，「外に出る，頭を越えて」など
の意味になることが多いので。

 英会話 footwork

Do you think fast-food restaurants will become more popular in the future?

関係代名詞（所有格）

直後には名詞が続きます。

whose：先行詞の所有物・付属物を説明します。

It is **quite a famous painting** (whose value is priceless).

This is a painting of **a dark room** (whose window is open).

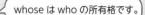

whose は who の所有格です。

そうね。だから先行詞は本来は「人」なんだけど、「物・事」も可能なのね。

3 【文法】日本語に合う英文になるように，関係代名詞を用いて空所に書きましょう。

(1) あなたは昨日自転車を盗まれた少年を知っていますか。

Do you know ＿＿＿＿＿ ＿＿＿＿＿ ＿＿＿＿＿ ＿＿＿＿＿ ＿＿＿＿＿ ＿＿＿＿＿

yesterday?

(2) あの男性だよ，お姉さんが有名な女優なのは。

That is ＿＿＿＿＿ ＿＿＿＿＿ ＿＿＿＿＿ ＿＿＿＿＿ a famous actress.

(3) 屋根の見えている家はベイリーさんの家です。

＿＿＿＿＿ ＿＿＿＿＿ ＿＿＿＿＿ ＿＿＿＿＿ ＿＿＿＿＿ ＿＿＿＿＿ just see is

Mr. Bailey's.

(4) 山頂が雪でおおわれているのはキリマンジャロ山です。　　　　　　　　(注)山頂：top

The mountain ＿＿＿＿＿ ＿＿＿＿＿ ＿＿＿＿＿ ＿＿＿＿＿ ＿＿＿＿＿

＿＿＿＿＿ is Mt. Kilimanjaro.

4 【表現】日本語に合う英文になるように，□□□から適切な語を選んで空所に書きましょう。

(1) 彼の自転車は私のとは対照的に古い。

His bike is old ＿＿＿＿＿ ＿＿＿＿＿ ＿＿＿＿＿ mine.

(2) ジューンは画家のモデルとして収入を得ていた。

June ＿＿＿＿＿ ＿＿＿＿＿ ＿＿＿＿＿ as an artist's model.

(3) フェルメールの最高傑作をじかに観てみませんか。

＿＿＿＿＿ don't you see his masterpieces ＿＿＿＿＿?

first-hand	living	a	made	with	contrast	in	why

5 【内容理解】本文の内容に合うように，□□□から適切な語を選んで空所に書きましょう。

In contrast with his ①(＿＿＿＿＿) today, many of his works became ②(＿＿＿＿＿) long after his death. Salvador Dali, a ③(＿＿＿＿＿) artist said, "Vermeer had the enthusiasm and ④(＿＿＿＿＿) to make ⑤(＿＿＿＿＿) is already perfect even more perfect."

what	distress	Spanish	valuable	reputation

No. Many people think fast food or junk food is unhealthy.

1【英語定義】次の英語の定義に相当する英単語を書きなさい。　〈5点×5〉

(1) building in which objects of art, history, science, etc. are displayed ＿＿＿＿＿＿

(2) woman who milks cows and works in a dairy ＿＿＿＿＿＿

(3) too valuable to be priced, important ＿＿＿＿＿＿

(4) something that was made or done with very great skill ＿＿＿＿＿＿

(5) be badly off, having very little money ＿＿＿＿＿＿

2【ストーリー・リテリング】教科書 p.92（Section 2）を 4 回音読した後，次の語句をすべて用いて本文を自分の言葉で再現しなさい。　〈8点〉

　　［使用語句］：Vermeer, the magician of light, another, color, Vermeer blue

＿＿＿＿＿＿＿＿＿＿＿＿＿＿＿＿＿＿＿＿＿＿＿＿＿＿＿＿＿＿＿＿＿＿＿＿

＿＿＿＿＿＿＿＿＿＿＿＿＿＿＿＿＿＿＿＿＿＿＿＿＿＿＿＿＿＿＿＿＿＿＿＿

＿＿＿＿＿＿＿＿＿＿＿＿＿＿＿＿＿＿＿＿＿＿＿＿＿＿＿＿＿＿＿＿＿＿＿＿

3【文法】日本語に合う英文になるように，空所に適切な語を書きなさい。　〈5点×4〉

(1) 私は彼女と話している少年を知っている。

　　I know a boy ＿＿＿＿ ＿＿＿＿ ＿＿＿＿ ＿＿＿＿ her.

(2) 私は母親が医者の少年を知っている。

　　I know a boy ＿＿＿＿ ＿＿＿＿ ＿＿＿＿ ＿＿＿＿ ＿＿＿＿.

(3) 私は彼女が愛する少年を知っている。

　　I know a boy ＿＿＿＿ ＿＿＿＿ ＿＿＿＿.

(4) これはその少年が私にくれたおもちゃだ。

　　This is the toy ＿＿＿＿ ＿＿＿＿ ＿＿＿＿ ＿＿＿＿ me.

4【文法】次の各組の文を関係代名詞を用いて 1 つの文にしなさい。　〈5点×4〉

(1) The woman was a Chinese. / I met her at the airport.

＿＿＿＿＿＿＿＿＿＿＿＿＿＿＿＿＿＿＿＿＿＿＿＿＿＿＿＿＿＿＿＿＿＿＿＿.

(2) Look at the boy and his dog. / They are running after a fox.

＿＿＿＿＿＿＿＿＿＿＿＿＿＿＿＿＿＿＿＿＿＿＿＿＿＿＿＿＿＿＿＿＿＿＿＿.

(3) I will show you the smartphone. / I bought it the day before yesterday.

＿＿＿＿＿＿＿＿＿＿＿＿＿＿＿＿＿＿＿＿＿＿＿＿＿＿＿＿＿＿＿＿＿＿＿＿.

(4) I'm so sorry to hear about the girl. / Her bike was stolen.

＿＿＿＿＿＿＿＿＿＿＿＿＿＿＿＿＿＿＿＿＿＿＿＿＿＿＿＿＿＿＿＿＿＿＿＿.

5 【内容理解】次の英文を読んで，下の問いに答えなさい。 〈計27点〉

Vermeer's nickname is "the magician of light." Look at "Milkmaid," one of his most important ①works. You can see the light from the window create soft shadow in the woman's face, hands, and clothing. Like this painting, there is often a window on the left side of his works. In this way, he mastered how to change our perception of figures with light.

Another characteristic is the use of color. Look at his most well-known work, "Girl with a Pearl Earring." The blue cloth ②(　　) the girl wears on her head is a Turkish turban. It shows that Turkish culture influenced art in Europe in the 17th century. Vermeer used the color called "Vermeer blue" to paint the turban. It was made from lapis lazuli, a deep-blue mineral. ③In ＿＿＿＿ ＿＿＿, it was almost as expensive as pure gold. Nevertheless, he used it abundantly for his paintings.

④In ＿＿＿＿ ＿＿＿ his reputation today, Vermeer didn't necessarily succeed as a painter in life. He had eleven children, and they had a lot of debt. One of his works was on a wall in a bakery. It is said that he handed over his works to pay for the bread. ⑤In ＿＿＿＿, he sold many of his works very cheaply to earn a living. Even about 200 years after his death, "Girl with a Pearl Earring" was sold for only two guilders and 30 cents. Many of his works gradually became valuable long after he died. Today, it is quite a famous painting ⑥(　　) value is priceless.

Salvador Dali, a Spanish artist said, "⑦Vermeer had the enthusiasm and distress to make what is already perfect even more perfect." Why don't you see his masterpieces first-hand?

(1) 下線部①の work と同じ意味の work を次のア～エから１つ選び，記号で答えなさい。 (3点)

　　ア　We saw Picasso's earlier works at the National Museum. (　　　)

　　イ　Stress is a part of work.

　　ウ　She works late at night for a living.

　　エ　All work and no play makes Jack a dull boy.

(2) ②と⑥の空所にそれぞれ入る that 以外の関係代名詞を書きなさい。 (3点×2)

　　②＿＿＿＿＿＿　　⑥＿＿＿＿＿＿

(3) ③が「あの頃は」，④が「～と比べて」，⑤が「実のところ」という意味になるように，□□□から適切な語を選んで書きなさい。 (3点×3)

　　③　In ＿＿＿＿＿＿ ＿＿＿＿＿＿

　　④　In ＿＿＿＿＿＿ ＿＿＿＿＿＿

　　⑤　In ＿＿＿＿＿＿

(4) 下線部⑦を日本語にしなさい。ただし，Vermeer は「フェルメール」と表記すること。 (5点)

＿＿＿＿＿＿＿＿＿＿＿＿＿＿＿＿＿＿＿＿＿＿＿＿＿＿＿＿＿＿＿＿＿＿＿＿＿

(5) 本文の内容に合うように，空所に入る語を書きなさい。 (4点)

　　ⓐ　In Vermeer's paintings, there is often a window on the ＿＿＿＿＿＿ side of his works.

　　ⓑ　The price of lapis lazuli, a deep-blue mineral was equal to that of pure ＿＿＿＿＿＿.

　　ⓒ　Johannes Vermeer is said to have handed over his works to pay for the ＿＿＿＿＿＿.

　　ⓓ　Even about 200 years after Vermeer's ＿＿＿＿＿＿, one of his paintings was sold at a low price.

1 【本文理解】音声を聞いて，区切りに気をつけて音読し，下の問いに答えましょう。

There are / about 8 million 7 hundred thousand living things / that exist on earth / now. // Humans are one of them. // While we are suffering / from world population
S V C

growth, / there are / lots of different animals / that are disappearing. // The International

Union / for Conservation of Nature / and Natural Resources / ── IUCN ── / listed /

13,482 kinds of animals / as endangered species / in 2018. //

Surprisingly, / 1,219 mammals / out of about 5,500 / are listed. // It means / that about
S   V

22% of ❶them / are becoming extinct, / such as Bengal tigers, / polar bears, / mountain

gorillas, / and black rhinos. // When you see these animals / at zoos, / you might imagine
S   V

❷them / living in the wild. // However, / some scientists say, / "In a few years, / zoos will
 O   C   S V

be the only places / G at which you can see these animals." //
C   （前置詞＋関係代名詞） S' V'   O'

(1) 下線部❶ them は何を指すのか，文中の語句で答えましょう。 ＿＿＿＿＿＿

(2) 下線部❷ them は何を指すのか，文中の語句で答えましょう。 ＿＿＿＿＿＿

2 【単語】次の語句の意味を調べて書きましょう。

(1) endangered 形（   ） (2) million* 名 形（   ）

(3) growth 名（   ） (4) union 名（   ）

(5) conservation 名（   ） (6) list(ed) 動（   ）

(7) surprisingly* 副（   ） (8) mammal(s) 名（   ）

(9) extinct 形（   ） (10) polar 形（   ）

(11) gorilla(s) 名（   ） (12) rhino(s) 名（   ）

Nice Fit 本文から抜き出しましょう。

世界的な人口増加 ＝（   ）（   ）（   ）

☕ **Coffee Break**

disappear（頭につけてつくる反意語）

disappear の dis- のように，頭につけて反意語になるものは，下記のようなものがあります。

un-, mis-, in-(im-), non-

英会話
footwork

Do you think computers will be used in more classes at school in the future?

→ Grammar

前置詞＋関係代名詞

関係代名詞が前置詞の目的語になる場合，前置詞を関係代名詞の前に移動させ，〈前置詞＋関係代名詞〉の形にすることができます。

Zoos will be the only **places** (at which you can see these animals).

It is also the **place** (on which nearly nine million kinds of living things exist).

関係代名詞(who, which)が前置詞の目的語になるとき，前置詞が関係代名詞の直前に置かれる場合があるんだ。

おもしろいわ。だから，English is the **subject** in which I am interested. なのよ。

3 【文法】日本語に合う英文になるように，適切な〈前置詞＋関係代名詞〉を書きましょう。

(1) これは，先週私があなたに話した雑誌だ。

This is the magazine ＿＿＿＿＿＿ ＿＿＿＿＿＿ I told you last week.

(2) 私たちには自慢のかわいい孫娘がいる。

We have a pretty granddaughter ＿＿＿＿＿＿ ＿＿＿＿＿＿ we are proud.

(3) あなたの曾祖父が生まれた町を知っていますか。

Do you know the town ＿＿＿＿＿＿ ＿＿＿＿＿＿ your great-grandfather was born?

(4) 私はマウナケア山の頂上に到達した日のことを決して忘れないだろう。

I'll never forget the day ＿＿＿＿＿＿ ＿＿＿＿＿＿ I reached the top of Mt. Mauna Kea.

4 【表現】日本語に合う英文になるように，□□□から適切な語を選んで空所に書きましょう。

(1) 彼らはまだ新型コロナウィルス感染症で苦しんでいる。

They are still ＿＿＿＿＿＿ ＿＿＿＿＿＿ COVID-19.

(2) 私たちの学校の生徒は5人のうち4人の割合で自転車通学している。

Four ＿＿＿＿＿＿ ＿＿＿＿＿＿ five students in our school go to school by bike.

| of | from | suffering | out |

5 【内容理解】本文の内容に合うように，次の質問に対する適切な答えをア〜エから選びましょう。

According to some scientists, what will zoos be like in a few years?　　　　（　　　）

ア　They will be centers for the scientific study of animals and their behavior.

イ　They will be places like *Jurassic Park*.

ウ　Most of them will be closed because of a sharp decrease in the number of animals in the wild.

エ　They will be the only places at which you can see 1,219 endangered mammals.

Yes. Students will be able to look up information online.

1 【本文理解】音声を聞いて，区切りに気をつけて音読し，下の問いに答えましょう。

According to some scientists, / our earth is facing / its sixth mass extinction. // The past
mass extinctions / were caused by volcanic eruptions, / natural climate changes, / and so
on. //

However, / the present ❶one / is almost entirely caused / by us — / humans. // Some
animals have been losing their habitats / because of deforestation, / overhunting, / or
poaching. // That's the biggest reason / G why mass extinction is going on / right now. //
(関係副詞)

Look at the "Red List Categories" / that IUCN published. // ❷It contains three red
categories / that show endangered species. // Surprisingly, / 80% of the animals / in Ueno
Zoo / are listed in these three categories. // It is alarming but true / that they are
disappearing / as fast as the last time / G when dinosaurs became extinct / about 65
(関係副詞)
million years ago. //

(1) 下線部❶ one は何を指すのか，文中の語で答えましょう。 _____

(2) 下線部❷ It は何を指すのか，文中の語で答えましょう。 _____

2 【単語】次の語句の意味を調べて書きましょう。

(1) mass 形( ) (2) extinction 名( )
(3) volcanic 形( ) (4) eruption(s) 名( )
(5) entirely 副( ) (6) habitat(s) 名( )
(7) deforestation 名( ) (8) overhunting 名( )
(9) poach(ing) 動( ) (10) categories < category 名( )
(11) publish(ed) 動( ) (12) alarming 形( )

 Nice Fit 火山の噴火によって引き起こされた
= ( ) ( ) ( ) ( ) ( )

Coffee Break
endanger（頭かお尻につけて名詞から動詞）
endanger の en- のように頭，またはお尻につけて名詞から動詞にするものに，下記のようなものがあります。
em-, -fy, -ize(-ise)

 英会話 footwork

 Do you think museums should be places that students can visit for free?

関係副詞①

後ろに「完全な文」を置いて，後ろから名詞句を説明します。

why：先行詞が「理由」(reason)の場合に用います。

when：先行詞が「時」(time / day など)の場合に用います。

That's the biggest **reason** (<u>why</u> mass extinction is going on right now).

They are disappearing as fast as the last **time** (<u>when</u> dinosaurs became extinct 65 million years ago).

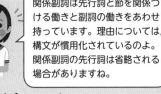

> 関係副詞は先行詞と節を関係づける働きと副詞の働きをあわせ持っています。理由については，構文が慣用化されているのよ。関係副詞の先行詞は省略される場合がありますね。

> 時間を表す先行詞に情報を追加する際には when によって関係詞節を導入するよ。基本形は the day[time] when … だね。そういえば，There comes a time when ～で始まる有名な曲があったような気がするよ。

3 【文法】日本語に合う英文になるように，(　　)内の語句を並べかえましょう。

(1) あなたが行かなかった理由を言いなさい。　Tell me (why / didn't / the reason / you / go).

Tell me _____ .

(2) 私たちが初めて会った日を覚えていますか。

(the day / we / when / remember / you / do) first met?

_____ first met?

(3) 彼が来なかった理由が知りたい。　(want / know / I / to / the reason / why) he didn't come.

_____ he didn't come.

(4) ベンは私が去った日にローマに来ました。　Ben arrived in Rome on (I / left / when / day / the).

Ben arrived in Rome on _____ .

4 【表現】日本語に合う英文になるように，□□から適切な語を選んで空所に書きましょう。

(1) 今日私たちはこの病気がウイルスによって引き起こされることを知っています。

We now know that this disease _____ _____ _____ viruses.

(2) しばらく待つことができますか，それともすぐに出なければいけませんか。

Can you wait a while or do you have to leave _____ _____ ?

now	right	caused	by	is

5 【内容理解】本文の内容に合う文はTを，合わない文はFを○で囲みましょう。

(1) Some scientists write that our earth is facing its sixth mass extinction. 　(T / F)

(2) The "Red List Categories" was published by World Wide Fund for Nature. 　(T / F)

(3) It is surprising that 65% of the animals in Ueno Zoo are listed as endangered species.

(T / F)

(4) Some animals are disappearing as fast as the last time when dinosaurs became extinct.

(T / F)

No. Museums need money to hold new events.

1 【本文理解】音声を聞いて，区切りに気をつけて音読し，下の問いに答えましょう。

Mass extinction is a serious problem / not only in foreign countries / but also in Japan. // Japan is one of the island countries / **G** where there exist many animals and plants / we cannot see in other places. // In fact, / 50% of mammals / on the land of Japan / inhabit only Japan. // If ❶they disappear from Japan, / it also means / that they will disappear on earth. //

In 2019, / the Ministry of the Environment / listed 3,676 kinds / of animals and plants / as endangered species. // Some of ❷them / are quite familiar to us, / for example, / Asiatic black bears, / storks, / sea otters, / dugongs, / and even killifish. //

The Environment Agency / has implemented artificial breeding programs, / feeding programs, / and so on. // That's **G** how we must protect endangered species / in our country. //

(1) 下線部❶ they は何を指すのか，文中の語句で答えましょう。　＿＿＿＿＿＿

(2) 下線部❷ them は何を指すのか，文中の語句で答えましょう。　＿＿＿＿＿＿

2 【単語】次の語句の意味を調べて書きましょう。

(1)	serious*	形(　　　)	(2)	exist*	動(　　　)
(3)	inhabit	動(　　　)	(4)	ministry	名(　　　)
(5)	stork(s)	名(　　　)	(6)	sea otter(s)	名(　　　)
(7)	dugong(s)	名(　　　)	(8)	killifish	名(　　　)
(9)	agency	名(　　　)	(10)	implement(ed)	動(　　　)
(11)	artificial*	形(　　　)	(12)	breeding	名(　　　)

 Nice Fit 絶滅危惧種を保護する ＝(　　　　) (　　　　) (　　　　)

Coffee Break

「冠詞」，あなどることなかれ！
45年ほど前の実話です。ある国立大学が入試で Bridge という題で自由英作文を出しました。入試問題正解解説書の執筆者であった英語母語話者の BJ(仮名)先生があえて模範解答として載せたのは，トランプゲームの内容でした。BJ 先生によると，Bridge は「コントラクトブリッジ」という意味で，「橋」という意味は A Bridge または The Bridge としなければならないのだそうです。大学側のミスということでした。

 英会話 footwork   Do you think that reading comic books is good for children?

関係副詞②

後ろに「完全な文」を置いて，後ろから名詞句を説明します。

where：先行詞が「場所」（place / house など）の場合に用います。

how：先行詞が「方法」（the way など）の場合に用いますが，

　　　how か the way の一方のみ使用可能。

Japan is one of the island **countries**

(<u>where</u> there exist many animals and plants)

we cannot see in other places.

That's (<u>how</u> we must protect endangered species in our country).

場所を表す先行詞の場合には，where を関係副詞として関係詞節を導入するよ。関係副詞の後ろには，完全な文が来るんだよね。

how には，方法の先行詞に情報を追加するという表現（×the way how）はないのね。

3 【文法】関係副詞（where あるいは how）を用いて，2 文を 1 文にしなさい。

(1) Recently I visited the city. I lived in the city when I was in Applause University.

Recently _____.

(2) This is the way. We wash our hands in this way.

This is _____.

(3) This is the town. I was born in this town.

This is _____.

(4) That was the way. He lost weight in that way.

That was _____.

4 【表現】日本語に合う英文になるように，□□□から適切な語を選んで空所に書きましょう。

(1) この機械は皿を洗うだけではなく，乾燥させます。

This machine _____ _____ washes the dishes _____ _____ dries them.

(2) 高橋商店では，コンピュータ，テレビ，ラジオなどを売っています。

Mr. Takahashi's store sells computers, televisions, radios, _____ _____ _____.

so	but	only	and	also	on	not

5 【内容理解】本文の内容に合う文は T を，合わない文は F を○で囲みましょう。

(1) Mass extinction is a serious problem mainly in Japan. （ T / F ）

(2) Half of the mammals on the land of Japan inhabit only in Japan. （ T / F ）

(3) The Ministry of the Environment listed 3,676 kinds of plants as endangered species.

（ T / F ）

(4) Asiatic black bears, storks, and sea otters are some of the endangered species in Japan.

（ T / F ）

Yes. There are comic books about history, science, and so on.

1 【本文理解】音声を聞いて，区切りに気をつけて音読し，下の問いに答えましょう。

We haven't always heard bad news / about endangered species. // One species was
S   V   O

excluded / from the list / in 2016 / because the number of them / was restored. // It was

the panda bear, / **G** which had been reduced / to only about 1,000 / by 1980. // One of the
(関係代名詞の非制限用法)

reasons was / that people destroyed its habitats / by cutting down bamboo trees. // ❶They

also hunted it / for its fur. // Later, / people established some sanctuaries, / **G** where
(関係副詞の非制限用法)

panda bears could live / and be protected. // All over the world, / actions to protect them /

such as crossbreeding, / or studying about them, / also worked well. //

In these ways, / humans threatened some animals / with extinction / in the past. // But
S   V   O

today / ❷they are saved from extinction / by humans. // What an irony / it is! //
                                                                   C   S   V

(1) 下線部❶ They は何を指すのか，文中の語で答えましょう。　＿＿＿＿＿＿

(2) 下線部❷ they 何を指すのか，文中の語句で答えましょう。　＿＿＿＿＿＿

2 【単語】次の語句の意味を調べて書きましょう。

(1) exclude(d) 　　動(　　　　　　)   (2) restore(d) 　　動(　　　　　　)

(3) fur 　　　　　名(　　　　　　)   (4) establish(ed) 　動(　　　　　　)

(5) sanctuaries＜sanctuary 名(　　　　　)   (6) crossbreed(ing) 　動(　　　　　　)

(7) threaten(ed) 　動(　　　　　　)   (8) irony 　　　　名(　　　　　　)

(9) save 　　　　動(　　　　　　)

Nice Fit 本文から抜き出しましょう。

生息地を破壊した＝(　　　　　) (　　　　　) (　　　　　)

Coffee Break

exclude（頭がエキスパーとで外に出す）
語の頭に ex-，ec-，es-，super-，sur- がつくと，「頭を越えて」「外に」の意味になります。

英会話 footwork   Do you hope students should take part in club activities at school?

• Grammar

関係代名詞と関係副詞の非制限用法

カンマ (,) に続いて用いられる関係代名詞・関係副詞の用法は「非制限用法」と呼ばれます。先行詞やカンマの前までの部分に補足の説明を加える働きをします。

「それは」,「そこで」などの言葉を補って考えるとわかりやすいでしょう。

It was the panda bear, (which had been reduced to only about 1,000 by 1980).

People established some sanctuaries, (where panda bears could live and be protected).

関係詞の前のカンマ (,) が非制限用法の目印ね。

そう，先行詞の補足説明を付加しているんだ。

3 【文法】日本語に合う英文になるように，which，where，または when を空所に入れましょう。

(1) 私たちはその村を訪れて，そこに2週間滞在したのである。

We visited the village, ＿＿＿＿＿＿ we stayed for two weeks.

(2) 彼らは感謝祭のパーティーをする予定で，それはとてもおもしろそうだ。

They will have a Thanksgiving party, ＿＿＿＿＿＿ sounds very interesting.

(3) 彼女は土曜日に祖母を訪問して，その時花火を見た。

She visited her grandmother on Saturday, ＿＿＿＿＿＿ she saw a fireworks display.

(4) 私のいとこは先週ケアンズから帰ってきたが，私はそれを知らなかった。

My cousin came back from Cairns last week, ＿＿＿＿＿＿ I didn't know.

4 【表現】日本語に合う英文になるように，□□□から適切な語を選んで空所に書きましょう。

(1) 相恩さんはその会合から締め出された。

Mr. So-on ＿＿＿＿＿ ＿＿＿＿＿ ＿＿＿＿＿ the meeting.

(2) このS字フックが役に立ったよ。

These S-shaped hooks ＿＿＿＿＿ ＿＿＿＿＿.

excluded	well	from	worked	was

5 【内容理解】本文の内容に合う文はTを，合わない文はFを○で囲みましょう。

(1) We have heard a piece of good news about endangered species. （ T / F ）

(2) For the last five years, there has been a sharp decrease in the number of panda bears.

（ T / F ）

(3) People established some sanctuaries, where panda bears were hunted for its fur. （ T / F ）

(4) Some animals once threatened by humans are saved from extinction by humans now.

（ T / F ）

No. Many students already have too much work to do.

1 【英語定義】次の英語の定義に相当する英単語を書きなさい。 〈5点×5〉

(1) one thousand thousand (1,000,000) _____

(2) plants' and animals' usual natural place and conditions of growth, home _____

(3) any of the class of animals which feed their young with milk from the breast _____

(4) area where by law it is forbidden to kill birds and animals, or rob their nests _____

(5) pass away _____

2 【ストーリー・リテリング】教科書 p.104（Section 1）を4回音読した後，次の語句をすべて用いて本文を自分の言葉で再現しなさい。 〈10点〉

［使用語句］：8 million 7 hundred thousand, disappearing, IUCN, 13,482, 2018

_____

_____

_____

3 【文法】次の各英文がほぼ同じ意味になるように，空所に適切な語を書きなさい。 〈5点×4〉

(1) This is the building which my father works in.

This is the building _____ _____ my father works.

(2) Wednesday and Thursday are the days on which I work from home.

Wednesday and Thursday are the days _____ I work from home.

(3) Their laziness is the reason for which they failed in business.

Their laziness is the reason _____ they failed in business.

(4) Tell me the way in which you learned to read Latin.

Tell me _____ you learned to read Latin.

4 【文法】日本語に合う英文になるように，（　）内の語句を並べかえなさい。 〈6点×3〉

(1) 土曜日は私が一番忙しくない日です。 Saturday (when / am / the day / is / I / least / busy).

Saturday _____.

(2) 君がそこへ行かねばならぬ理由はない。

There is (no / there / should / why / you / go / reason).

There is _____.

(3) ポチは涼しい木陰にすわった。 Pochi sat (in / where / cool / of a tree / was / it / the shade).

Pochi sat _____.

5 【内容理解】次の英文を読んで，下の問いに答えなさい。 〈計27点〉

According to some scientists, our earth is facing its sixth mass extinction. The past mass extinctions were caused by volcanic eruptions, natural climate changes, ①(____) (____) (____).

However, the present one is almost entirely caused by us — humans. Some animals have been losing their habitats because of deforestation, overhunting, or poaching. That's the biggest reason ②(____) mass extinction is going on right now.

Look at the "Red List Categories" that IUCN published. It contains three red categories that show endangered species. Surprisingly, 80% of the animals in Ueno Zoo are listed in these three categories. It is alarming but true that they are disappearing as fast as the last time ③(____) dinosaurs became extinct 65 million years ago.

④Mass extinction is a serious problem not only in foreign countries but also in Japan. Japan is one of the island countries ⑤(____) there exist many animals and plants we cannot see in other places. In fact, 50% of mammals on the land of Japan inhabit only Japan. If they disappear from Japan, ⑥(on / it / will / they / disappear / that / earth / also means).

In 2019, the Ministry of the Environment listed 3,676 kinds of animals and plants as endangered species. Some of them are quite familiar to us, ⑦(____) (____), Asiatic black bears, storks, sea otters, dugongs, and even killifish.

The Environment Agency has implemented artificial breeding programs, feeding programs, and so on. That's ⑧(____) we must protect endangered species in our country.

(1) 次の英単語と発音が同じでスペリングの異なる語を本文中から抜き出しなさい。 (1点×8)

ⓐ sum _____　　ⓑ hour _____　　ⓒ passed _____

ⓓ won _____　　ⓔ there _____　　ⓕ write _____

ⓖ read（過去形）_____　　ⓗ sea _____

(2) ①が「〜など」，⑦が「例にとって見れば」という意味になるように，適切な語を□□□から選んで書きなさい。 (2点×2)

①_____ _____ _____　　⑦_____ _____

| instant | example | for | on | so | and | force |

(3) ②，③，⑤，⑧の空所にそれぞれ入る適切な関係副詞を書きなさい。 (1点×4)

②_____　　③_____　　⑤_____　　⑧_____

(4) 下線部④を日本語にしなさい。 (4点)

_____

(5) 下線部⑥の（　　）内の語句を，「そういった希少動物が地球上から消え去るということをも意味する」という意味になるように，並べかえて書きなさい。 (4点)

(　　　　　　　　　　　　　　　　　　　　　　　　　　　　　)

(6) 本文の内容に合う文はTを，合わない文はFを○で囲みましょう。 (3点)

ⓐ The last five extinctions on earth were caused only by volcanic eruptions. （ T / F ）

ⓑ Half of the mammals on the land of Japan live only in Japan. （ T / F ）

ⓒ Dinosaurs became extinct about 65,000,000 years ago. （ T / F ）

1 【本文理解】音声を聞き，区切りに気をつけて音読し，下の問いに答えましょう。

Have you ever seen *Star Wars* or *Harry Potter*? // You may be surprised / to see "Yoda"

S　　V　　　　　　　　　　　　　　　　　　　　　O

and "Goblin" / on the screen. // **❶**They were created / with "special makeup." // It is often

S　　　　　　V

used for visual arts, / such as movies or dramas / to create imaginary creatures. //

Special makeup is also used / to create animals / which look like real ones. // Look at

the picture below. // **G** If someone tells you / that this is a fake gorilla, / you may not

（条件を表す副詞節）

believe **❷**it. // This is a gorilla suit / made by using special makeup / for a movie. // It has

scenes / where a zookeeper character and a gorilla / sit and sleep / side by side. // Special

makeup / makes difficult scenes / possible. //

S　　　　　V　　　　　　O　　　　　C

(1) 下線部**❶**They は誰を指すのか，文中の語句で答えましょう。　　＿＿＿＿＿＿

(2) 下線部**❷**it が指す内容を，簡潔な日本語で答えましょう。　　＿＿＿＿＿＿

2 【単語】次の語句の意味を調べて書きましょう。

(1) war(s)* 名(　　　　　) (2) screen* 名(　　　　　)

(3) special* 形(　　　　　) (4) makeup 名(　　　　　)

(5) visual 形(　　　　　) (6) drama(s) 名(　　　　　)

(7) imaginary 形(　　　　　) (8) creature* 名(　　　　　)

(9) below* 副(　　　　　) (10) fake 形(　　　　　)

(11) scene(s)* 名(　　　　　) (12) zookeeper 名(　　　　　)

Nice Fit 本文から抜き出しましょう。

にせ物のゴリラ＝(　　　　　) (　　　　　) (　　　　　)

Coffee Break

本文中の side by side のように語頭と同一の韻を繰り返すものを「頭韻」といいます。最初に決めた志を最後まで持ち続けよという英国発の標語を紹介します。
——Keep Calm and Carry On. 頭韻がバッチリ決まってますね。——冷静に継続せよ。

 英会話 footwork

Do you think more foreign students will come to Japan in the future?

• Grammar

条件を表す副詞節

if(もし〜ならば)などで始まる節を「条件を表す副詞節」と言います。

条件を表す副詞節では，未来のことも現在形を用いて表します。

when など，時を表す場合も同様です。

If someone <u>tells</u> you that this is a fake gorilla, you may not believe it.

Unless special makeup <u>is used</u>, imaginary creatures cannot be created.

時・条件を表す副詞節の中では，未来のことであっても現在形を用います。

オッケー，I'll tell you the truth when I see (× will see) you next time. ということで。

---

3 【文法】日本語に合う英文になるように，(　　　)内の語句を並べかえましょう。(1語不要)

(1) もし雨が降るようなら家にいるつもりです。　We'll (will rain / home / rains / it / stay / if).

We'll _____.

(2) 帰宅してからまた会おうね。　I'll see you (home / I / get / when / will get).

I'll see you _____.

(3) 明日雪が降れば，スキーに行きます。　I will go skiing (will snow / snows / tomorrow / it / if).

I will go skiing _____.

(4) 今珈琲を飲まないと冷たくなるよ。

Your coffee will get cold (you / will drink / now / it / drink / unless).

Your coffee will get cold _____.

---

4 【表現】日本語に合う英文になるように，□□□から適切な語を選んで空所に書きましょう。

(1) 私たちはオレンジ，レモンなどたくさんの果物をカリフォルニアから輸入しています。

We import a lot of fruit, _____ _____ oranges and lemons from California.

(2) あの2人は並んで写真をとった。

Those two stood _____ _____ _____ for the photo.

| side | as | by | such | side |

---

5 【内容理解】本文の内容に合うように，次の質問に対する適切な答えをア〜エから選びましょう。

Why has the gorilla suit been made by using special makeup?　　　　　(　　　)

ア　Because the special makeup artist has always been a big fan of *Planet of the Apes*.

イ　Because the real gorilla is pregnant and she is going to have a baby soon.

ウ　Because it has suddenly been decided that another gorilla is needed for the movie.

エ　Because the movie has scenes where a zookeeper character sits and sleeps next to a gorilla.

Yes. They want to learn more about Japan by living here.

1 【本文理解】音声を聞いて，区切りに気をつけて音読し，下の問いに答えましょう。

G If there were human-like animals, / we could ask them / to act in movies. // In (仮定法過去) reality, / we need to create ❶them. // The following is the procedure / for transforming a person / into a mermaid. //

1. / First, / place colored contact lenses / on the model's eyes. // Conceal her eyebrows / and protect her hair / with a rubber wig cap. //

2. / Next, / cover her head / with a mermaid wig / prepared in advance / and fix ❷it with glue. // Put artificial ears / and then / apply a rubber piece / along her forehead. //

3. / Last, / blend the edges / of the rubber material / and apply makeup / on her entire face. // This is a completed mermaid look. //

If you want to be a special makeup artist, / you can learn ❸it / at makeup school. //
S´ V´   O´   S   V   O

(1) 下線部❶ them は何を指すのか，文中の語句で答えましょう。　　　　＿＿＿＿＿＿

(2) 下線部❷ it は何を指すのか，文中の語句で答えましょう。　　　　　＿＿＿＿＿＿

(3) 下線部❸ it は何になるためのものか，文中の語句で答えましょう。　＿＿＿＿＿＿

2 【単語】次の語句の意味を調べて書きましょう。

(1)	reality	名( )	(2)	procedure	名( )
(3)	transform(ing)	動( )	(4)	mermaid	名( )
(5)	lens(es)	名( )	(6)	conceal	動( )
(7)	eyebrow(s)	名( )	(8)	rubber	名( )
(9)	wig	名( )	(10)	cap	名( )
(11)	in advance	( )	(12)	apply	動( )
(13)	along	前( )	(14)	forehead	名( )
(15)	blend	動( )	(16)	edge(s)	名( )

 彼女の顔全体に化粧を施す

= ( ) ( ) ( ) ( ) ( ) ( )

☕ **Coffee Break**

reality（お尻につけて形容詞から名詞）
reality の -ity のように，お尻につけて形容詞から名詞にするものに，下記のようなものがあります。
-ty, -ness

英会話 footwork

Should people buy things that are good for the environment, even when they are expensive?

仮定法過去

〈If＋主語＋動詞の過去形〜，主語＋would＋動詞の原形〉で「もし〜ならば，…なのに」という意味を表し，現在の事実と異なることを述べるときに用います。

主節で使われる助動詞としては，ほかに could や might などがあります。

If there **were** human-like animals, we <u>could ask</u> them to act in movies.

If I **were** a special makeup artist, I <u>would create</u> an imaginary mermaid figure.

仮定法過去は，視点を現在において「仮に〜としたらどうする」という仮想の状況を設定した言い方というわけだね。

視点は現在にあるけれど，過去形を用いることから仮定法過去と呼ばれているのよね。仮定法過去では，主語が I のときでも be 動詞は were を用いるのね。

3 【文法】日本語に合う英文になるように，（　　）内の語を適切な形にかえて空所に書きましょう。

(1) もし健康なら，私は渋谷に買い物に行くのですがねえ。　（be）

　　If I ＿＿＿＿＿＿ healthy, I would go shopping in Shibuya.

(2) もし彼女がここに来たら，私はいくつか質問するのだがなあ。　（come, ask）

　　If she ＿＿＿＿＿＿ here, I ＿＿＿＿＿＿ ＿＿＿＿＿＿ some questions.

(3) もし十分な時間があれば，私はハワイに行くかもしれないのですが。　（have, go）

　　If I ＿＿＿＿＿＿ enough time, I ＿＿＿＿＿＿ ＿＿＿＿＿＿ to Hawaii.

(4) もし彼女の住所を知っていたら，私は彼女に手紙を書くことができるのだが。　（write, know）

　　I ＿＿＿＿＿＿ ＿＿＿＿＿＿ to her if I ＿＿＿＿＿＿ her address.

4 【表現】日本語に合う英文になるように，＿＿＿から適切な語を選んで空所に書きましょう。

(1) 磯路さんは若く見えるが，実際は50歳を越えている。

　　Mr. Isoji looks young, but ＿＿＿＿＿＿ ＿＿＿＿＿＿ he is past fifty.

(2) 強烈な日差しと湿気のせいで，ビニールハウスは巨大な蒸し風呂のような暑さだった。

　　A hot sun and the humidity ＿＿＿＿＿＿ the plastic greenhouse ＿＿＿＿＿＿ a giant steam bath.

> into　　reality　　in　　transformed

5 【内容理解】本文の内容に合う文はTを，合わない文はFを〇で囲みましょう。

(1) Since there aren't human like animals, we cannot ask them to act in movies.　（ T / F ）

(2) A mermaid is a man who has a fish's tail instead of legs and who lives in the sea. （ T / F ）

(3) You cover the model's head with a prepared mermaid wig and fix it with Scotch tapes.

　　（ T / F ）

(4) To become a special makeup artist, you can learn it at computer animation school.

　　（ T / F ）

Yes. People need to start doing more to protect the environment.

1 【本文理解】音声を聞いて，区切りに気をつけて音読し，下の問いに答えましょう。

There are many special makeup artists / in Japan. // They may say, / " **G** I wish / I could

（V）　　　　　　　　　　　　　　　　　　　　　（S）

be a world-famous special makeup artist." // In 2018, / one of **❶**them won the Academy　　　　　　　　（仮定法過去）

Award / for Best Makeup and Hairstyling. // His name is Kazu Hiro. //

When he was in senior high school, / he read a magazine article / about Dick Smith. //

He was a well-known special makeup artist / in the world. // Kazu Hiro had an interest in

it / and sent a letter to him. // Kazu Hiro soon got a reply / from Smith. // Smith wrote: /

"Do you speak and read English / as well as you write **❷**it? // Your letter is perfect." //

After that, / Kazu Hiro studied English hard / to ask **❸**him questions / and understand

his advice. // This exchange of letters / changed his life. // At 26, / his dream to work in

（S）　　　　　　　　　　　　　　　（V）　　　（O）　　　　　　　　　　（S）

Hollywood / came true. //

（V）（C）

(1) 下線部**❶** them は誰を指すのか，文中の語句で答えましょう。　　＿＿＿＿＿＿

(2) 下線部**❷** it は何を指すのか，文中の語で答えましょう。　　＿＿＿＿＿＿

(3) 下線部**❸** him は誰を指すのか，文中の語句で答えましょう。　　＿＿＿＿＿＿

2 【単語】次の語句の意味を調べて書きましょう。

(1) artist(s)　　　　名(　　　　　　)　　(2) world-famous*　　形(　　　　　　)

(3) academy　　　　名(　　　　　　)　　(4) award　　　　　名(　　　　　　)

(5) hairstyling　　　名(　　　　　　)　　(6) article*　　　　名(　　　　　　)

(7) well-known*　　形(　　　　　　)　　(8) interest*　　　名(　　　　　　)

(9) reply*　　　　　動(　　　　　　)　　(10) A as well as B*　前(　　　　　　)

(11) exchange*　　　名(　　　　　　)　　(12) Hollywood　　　名(　　　　　　)

Nice Fit　ディック・スミスの雑誌記事

= (　　　　　　)(　　　　　　)(　　　　　　)(　　　　　　)(　　　　　　)(　　　　　　)

☕ **Coffee Break**

exchange（頭がエキスパーと外に出る）

こんな覚え方どうですか？　sur-, ex-, ec-, es-, super- が頭につくと，「外に出る，頭を越えて」などの
意味になることが多いので。

Do you think that people these days put too much personal information online?

• Grammar

I wish＋仮定法過去

〈I wish＋主語＋動詞の過去形～〉で現実とは異なる願望を表します。

<u>I wish</u> I <u>could be</u> a world famous special makeup artist.

<u>I wish</u> I <u>could write</u> letters in English like Kazu Hiro.

「～であったらいのに」という気持ちが表現されているはね。

願望を表す仮定法過去の典型表現だね。仮定法を使うと，いくらでも高望みができるね。

3 【文法】日本語に合う英文になるように，（　　　）内の語句を並べかえましょう。

(1) 彼が車の運転ができればなあ。　(wish / a car / he / drive / I / could).

_____.

(2) ドイツ語が上手にしゃべれるならなあ。　(well / German / speak / could / I / wish / I).

_____.

(3) もしも私が鳥ならばなあ。　(bird / wish / a / I / were / I).

_____.

(4) ああ，うちらに百万ドルあったらなあ。　(wish / a million / dollars / we / had / we).

_____.

4 【表現】日本語に合う英文になるように，□□□から適切な語を選んで空所に書きましょう。

(1) 家賃は前払いでお願いいたします。

Please pay the rent ＿＿＿＿＿＿ ＿＿＿＿＿＿.

(2) あしながおじさんは私たちに着物はもちろん食べ物もくれた。

Daddy-Long-Leg gave us food ＿＿＿＿＿＿ ＿＿＿＿＿＿ ＿＿＿＿＿＿ clothes.

(3) まるで夢が実現したようだ。

It's like a ＿＿＿＿＿＿ ＿＿＿＿＿＿ ＿＿＿＿＿＿.

| advance | in | as | well | as | true | come | dream |

5 【内容理解】本文の内容に合うように，次の質問に対する適切な答えをア～エから選びましょう。

After getting a reply from Dick Smith, why did Kazu Hiro study English hard?　(　　　)

ア　Because he wanted to read a magazine article about Smith.

イ　Because he wanted to ask Smith questions and understand his advice.

ウ　Because he had an interest in the special makeup artist and wanted to send a letter to Smith.

エ　Because there were too many special makeup artists in Japan.

No. Most people are very careful about what they put online.

1 【本文理解】音声を聞いて，区切りに気をつけて音読し，下の問いに答えましょう。

In the United States, / Kazu Hiro worked on / many films. // Although he had been nominated / for the Academy Award / twice, / he had never won **❶**it. // At 48, / he had a big chance. // Gary Oldman, / the principal actor / in the film *Darkest Hour*, / thought Kazu Hiro was the only person / Oldman wanted to do his makeup. // Oldman also said, / "If **❷**he declined, / I wasn't going to take the role." // That's why he worked on this film. // "Gary Oldman looks / **G** as if he were the real Winston Churchill!" / said people who

（仮定法過去）

watched it. // It made Kazu Hiro / the first Japanese makeup artist / to win the Academy Award. //

Kazu Hiro said / to young people, / "Understand the thing / you want to do, / make efforts for **❸**it, / and believe in yourself. // Don't be afraid / of making mistakes. // Mistakes are an important part / of success. // Don't run away / from yourself. //

S   V   C

Concentrate / on your true passion." //

(1) 下線部❶ it は何を指すのか，文中の語句で答えましょう。＿＿＿＿＿

(2) 下線部❷ he 誰を指すのか，文中の語句で答えましょう。＿＿＿＿＿

(3) 下線部❸ it は何を指すのか，文中の語句で答えましょう。＿＿＿＿＿

2 【単語】次の語句の意味を調べて書きましょう。

(1) film(s)* 名( ) (2) nominate(d) 動( )

(3) principal* 形( ) (4) actor* 名( )

(5) decline(d) 動( ) (6) role* 名( )

(7) That's why ～* ( ) (8) as if ～ ( )

(9) make efforts* ( ) (10) believe in ～* ( )

(11) concentrate 動( ) (12) passion* 名( )

Nice Fit 失敗を恐れてはいけない

= ( ) ( ) ( ) ( ) ( ) .

☕ **Coffee Break**

英会話の極意

外国語は口を開けば間違えるもの。私の話題なんかと謙遜せず，気楽に間違えながら進んでいきましょう。小生もアメリカのお店で raisin(干しブドウ)を頼んだら razor(安全かみそり)を手渡された経験がありますよ。

英会話 footwork

Do you believe that, in the future, more people will use robots to clean their homes?

Grammar

as if＋仮定法過去

〈as if＋主語＋動詞の過去形〜〉で「まるで／あたかも〜のように」という意味を表します。

Gary Oldman looks <u>as if</u> he <u>were</u> the real Winston Churchill.

My friend looks happy <u>as if</u> his dream <u>came</u> true.

仮定法特有の表現だね。

「〜であるかのように」という意味が出ます。〜内で用いられる動詞は，were，knew，lived など，通例状態動詞ですね。

3 【文法】日本語に合う英文になるように，（　　）内の語句を並べかえましょう。

(1) 彼はまるでその事故について何でも知っているかのように話す。

He (if / about / as / everything / knew / he / talks) the accident.

He _____ the accident.

(2) スクルージはまるで左ききのような書き方をする。

Scrooge writes (he / left-handed / if / were / as).

Scrooge writes _____.

(3) 彼は中国語をネイティブスピーカーのようにすらすらと話す。

He speaks Chinese as fluently (a native / he / if / were / as).

He speaks Chinese as fluently _____.

4 【表現】日本語に合う英文になるように，□□から適切な語を選んで空所に書きましょう。

(1) 英男は広子の感情を傷つけるのではないかと不安に思った。

Hideo _____ _____ _____ _____ Hiroko's feelings.

(2) 重要な問題に集中して取り組もう。

Let's _____ _____ the important issues.

| on | hurting | afraid | was | of | concentrate |

5 【内容理解】本文の内容に合う文はTを，合わない文はFを○で囲みましょう。

(1) Before Kazu Hiro won the Academy Award, he had been nominated for it two times.

(T / F)

(2) At 48, Kazu Hiro became the first Japanese makeup artist to win the Academy Award.

(T / F)

(3) Gary Oldman played the role of Winston Churchill in the film *Darkest Hour*. (T / F)

(4) Gary Oldman thought Kazu Hiro was the only person he wanted to do his makeup.

(T / F)

Yes. We're too busy. Also, robots can clean better than people.

75

1 【英語定義】次の英語の定義に相当する英単語を書きなさい。 〈5点×5〉

(1) existing only in the mind, unreal, (*for example*) such as a dragon _____

(2) woman with a fish's tail in place of legs in children's stories _____

(3) center of the US film industry _____

(4) strong feeling or enthusiasm, especially of love, hate or anger _____

(5) make up one's mind _____

2 【ストーリー・リテリング】教科書 p.124 (Section 3) を4回音読した後，次の語句をすべて用いて本文を自分の言葉で再現しなさい。 〈10点〉

[使用語句]：2018, Kazu Hiro, senior high school, Dick Smith, his dream

_____

_____

_____

3 【文法】日本語に合う英文になるように，空所に適切な語を書きなさい。 〈5点×4〉

(1) もし彼に十分なお金があれば，新車を買えるのに。

If he _____ enough money, he _____ buy a new car.

(2) もし私がジェット機なら，空を音速で空を飛ぶだろうに。

If I _____ a jet plane, I _____ fly in the sky at the speed of sound.

(3) もし彼女がここにいれば，それを聞いて喜ぶだろうになあ。

If she _____ here, she _____ _____ glad to hear it.

(4) 夫が家に帰って来る前に仕事をすませておきます。

I'll finish the work before my husband _____ home.

4 【文法】日本語に合う英文になるように，（ ）内の語を並べかえなさい。 〈6点×3〉

(1) 彼はまるで何でも知っているかのように話す。 He (as / everything / if / knew / he / talks).

He _____.

(2) たんまり僕にお金があればなあ。 I (had / money / enough / I / wish).

I _____.

(3) もし明朝風が強くなかったら，バンジージャンプをやろう。

Let's do bungee jump (windy / not / is / it / if / morning / tomorrow).

Let's do bungee jump _____.

5 【内容理解】 次の英文を読んで，下の問いに答えなさい。 〈計27点〉

There are many special makeup artists in Japan. They may say, "I wish I ①(can) be a world-famous special makeup artist." In 2018, one of them won the Academy Award for Best Makeup and Hairstyling. His name is Kazu Hiro.

When he was in senior high school, he read a magazine article about Dick Smith. He was a well-known special makeup artist in the world. Kazu Hiro had an interest in it and sent a letter to him. Kazu Hiro soon got a reply ②(   ) Smith. Smith wrote: "③Do you speak and read English as well as you write it? Your letter is perfect."

After that, Kazu Hiro studied English hard to ask him questions and understand his advice. ④(letters / changed / of / his / life / this exchange). At 26, his dream to work in Hollywood ⑤(   )(   ).

In the United States, Kazu Hiro worked on many films. Although he had been nominated for the Academy Award twice, he had never won it. At 48, he had a big chance. Gary Oldman, the principal actor in the film *Darkest Hour*, thought Kazu Hiro was the only person Oldman wanted to do his makeup. Oldman also said, "⑥If he declined, I wasn't going to take the role." That's the reason ⑦(   ) he worked on this film. "Gary Oldman looks as if he ⑧(be) the real Winston Churchill!" said people who watched it. It made Kazu Hiro the first Japanese makeup artist to win the Academy Award.

Kazu Hiro said to young people, "Understand ⑨the thing you want to do, make efforts for it, and believe in yourself. ⑩ 間違いを犯すのをこわがっていてはいけません。 Mistakes are an important part of success. Don't run away from yourself. Concentrate ⑪(   ) your true passion."

(1) 下線部①と⑧の（　　）内の語を適切な形に変えて書きなさい。 (1点×2)

　　① can → _____　　⑧ be → _____

(2) ②と⑪の空所に入る適切な前置詞を [　　] から1つずつ選んで書きなさい。 (1点×2)

　　② (　　　　　　　) Smith　　⑪ Concentrate (　　　　　　　)

for	to	in	on	between	from	through	against	under

(3) 下線部③と⑥をそれぞれ日本語にしなさい。 (3点×2)

　　③_____　　⑥_____

(4) ④の（　　）内の語句を並べかえて，「この手紙のやりとりによって彼の人生が変わった」という意味になるようにしなさい。 (3点)

　　(　　　　　　　　　　　　　　　　　　　　　　　　　　　　　　　　　　　　　).

(5) 下線部⑤に2語補い，文意が通じるようにしなさい。 (3点)

　　… his dream to work in Hollywood (　　　　　　　)(　　　　　　　).

(6) 下線部⑦に入る適切な関係副詞を書きなさい。 (　　　　　　) (2点)

(7) 下線部⑨を別の英語1語で書きかえなさい。 (　　　　　　) (3点)

(8) ⑩の空所 [　　] にある日本文を英語に直しなさい。 (3点)

_____.

(9) 本文の内容に合うように，次の質問に対する適切な答えを完成させなさい。 (3点)

After getting a reply from Smith, why did Kazu Hiro study English hard?

　　—— In order _____ ask him _____ and understand his _____.

由美のメール

▶p.133

---

1 【本文理解】区切りに気をつけて音読し，下の問いに答えましょう。

Subject: Greetings from Japan //

Dear Mr. and Mrs. Brown, //

My name is Kimura Yumi / and I am writing you from Japan. // I will be staying at your

place / from December 20th. // I would like to thank you / in advance / for having me. //

This is my first time / to travel abroad, / so I am a bit nervous. // I like cooking and

playing ice hockey / in my free time. // I heard / you have a son / who is five years old. //

❶He plays hockey as well. //

While I'm in Canada, / I would like to do / some volunteer work / and to go watch an

NHL game. // I'm looking forward / to meeting you. //

Sincerely yours, //

Kimura Yumi //

---

(1) 下線部**❶** He は誰を指すのか，文中の語句で答えましょう。　　　　　　　　　　　　

---

2 【単語】次の語句の意味を調べて書きましょう。

(1) greeting(s)　　　名(　　　　　　　)　　(2) hockey　　　　名(　　　　　　　)

(3) NHL　　　　　名(　　　　　　　)　　(4) look forward to ～ing　(　　　　　　　)

Nice Fit 本文から抜き出しましょう。

あらかじめ，前もって = (　　　　　　　)(　　　　　　　)

✉ ⟨e メールQ & A

Q 絵文字は使ってもよいでしょうか？

A カジュアルなメールで使いたいのであれば OK ですが，多少ともきちんとしたメールを書きたい場合は
お勧めしません。記号や特殊文字を使った顔文字の例を以下にいくつか挙げておきます（頭を左に90度傾
けないとわかりにくいかもしれません）。

:)　Happy Face(幸せ顔)　　　　　　　　:-D Big Smile(ビッグスマイル)

:(　Sad Face(悲しい顔)　　　　　　　　:-O Shocked(ショック)

;)　Winking(ウィンク)　　　　　　　　:-P Sticking Tongue Out(舌だし)

:-) Happy With Nose(鼻のある幸せ顔)

アムステルダム国立美術館にはフェルメールの「牛乳を注ぐ女」やレンブラントの「夜警」が所蔵されています。上の例を参考にして，アムステルダム国立美術館にEメールを書いてみましょう。

＊アムステルダム国立美術館：info@rijiksmuseum.nl

1　Subject（件名）を書きましょう。

2　最初は To Rijiks Museum で始めましょう。

3　自己紹介（好きなことや趣味について）書きましょう。

4　用件を書きましょう。

5　結びの文を書きましょう。

6　最後に自分の名前を書きましょう。

---

3 【文法】日本文に合う英文になるように，（　　）内の動詞を適切な形にかえて空所に書きましょう。

(1) 曽根さんは食べることが大好きです。　(eat)

Miss Sone is very ＿＿＿＿＿＿ ＿＿＿＿＿＿ ＿＿＿＿＿＿.

(2) ぼくは明朝早くニューヨークへ飛ぶ予定です。　(fly)

I'm ＿＿＿＿＿＿ ＿＿＿＿＿＿ New York early tomorrow morning.

(3) 熱気球に乗って空から町をながめるのは，ぼく初めてなんです。　(ride in)

This is my first time ＿＿＿＿＿＿ ＿＿＿＿＿＿ ＿＿＿＿＿＿ a hot-air balloon and look down on my town from the sky.

4 【表現】日本語に合う英文になるように，□□□から適切な語を選んで空所に書きましょう。

(1) オアフかマウイで暮らしたいものだが。

I ＿＿＿＿＿＿ ＿＿＿＿＿＿ ＿＿＿＿＿＿ ＿＿＿＿＿＿ in Oahu or Maui.

(2) 72時間前にご連絡ください。

Get in touch with me seventy-two hours ＿＿＿＿＿＿ ＿＿＿＿＿＿.

(3) ロンドンに戻るのを待ち遠しく思っています。

I'm ＿＿＿＿＿＿ ＿＿＿＿＿＿ ＿＿＿＿＿＿ ＿＿＿＿＿＿ back to London.

going	advance	live	would	in	looking	to	like	to	forward

5 【内容理解】本文の内容に合う文はTを，合わない文はFを○で囲みましょう。

(1) Kimura Yumi will be staying at Mr. and Mrs. Brown's place till December 20th.　(T / F)

(2) Kimura Yumi has never been abroad, so she is a bit worried.　(T / F)

(3) Kimura Yumi likes cooking and playing ice hockey in her free time.　(T / F)

(4) Kimura Yumi would like to do some volunteer work and to go watch an NBA game.

(T / F)

1 【本文理解】区切りに気をつけて音読し，下の問いに答えましょう。

Subject: Thank you for your e-mail //

Dear Yumi, //

Thank you for your e-mail. // Our son Bob says / he wants to play ice hockey / with you. //

He is good at playing ❶it. // We hope / you'll enjoy it / with him. // We are planning / to go

watch an NHL game / during your homestay. // Let's go together! //

Actually, / we have pets: / a rabbit and a cat. // I attached / some pictures of them and

ours / to this mail. // We hope / you will like ❷them. //
<small>S   V   O</small>

We have a favor / to ask you. // We would like to know / how to cook sukiyaki. // Could

you help us / cook it? // We're looking forward / to seeing you / too. :) //

Sincerely yours, //

Julie Brown //

---

(1) 下線部❶ it は何を指すのか，文中の語句で答えましょう。　　　　＿＿＿＿＿＿＿

(2) 下線部❷ them は何を指すか，文中の語句で答えましょう。　　　　＿＿＿＿＿＿＿

2 【単語】次の語句の意味を調べて書きましょう。

(1) attach(ed)　　　　動(　　　　　　　　)　　(2) favor　　　　　名(　　　　　　　)

Nice Fit 本文から抜き出しましょう。

あなたにお願いしたいことがあるのですが。 =(　　　　　　)(　　　　　　)(　　　　　　)

(　　　　　　)(　　　　　　)(　　　　　　)(　　　　　　).

3 【文法】日本文に合う英文になるように，空所に適当な前置詞を書きましょう。

(1) 私は夏休み3週間入院していた。

I was in hospital for three weeks ＿＿＿＿＿＿ the summer vacation.

(2) 彼女はカルガリーへアイススケートをしに行った。

She went ice skating ＿＿＿＿＿＿ Calgary.

(3) 警察が到着するまでこの部屋をそのままにしておきましょう。

Let's leave the room as it is ＿＿＿＿＿＿ the police arrive.

①お尋ねしたいことがあります。　I have a question about …

②ちょっと教えてほしいことが。　There's something I'd like you to help me with.

③ご教授ください。　I would be very grateful for your advice.

④何か特別なイベントはあるでしょうか。　Will there be any special events?

⑤開館時間を教えてください。　Could you tell me what your business hours are?

⑥お体にお気をつけて。　Look after yourself.

⑦前からニューヨークへ行ってみたかった。　I've always wanted to go to New York.

4【表現】日本語に合う英文になるように，☐☐から適切な語を選んで空所に書きましょう。

(1) （掲示などで）店内で物を食べないでください。

　　_____ _____ _____ not eating in the store.

(2) その時とったお二人の写真を添付します。

　　I'm _____ _____ _____ we took of you two at that time.

(3) ココダ・ストリートへの行き方を教えてもらえますか。

　　Can you _____ _____ _____ _____ get to the Kokoda Street?

| to | photo | for | tell | attaching | thank | how | a | you | me |

5【内容理解】本文の内容に合う文は T を，合わない文は F を○で囲みましょう。

(1) Mr. and Mrs. Brown's son Bob wants to play ice hockey with Kimura Yumi.　　　　（ T / F ）

(2) Kimura Yumi and her host family are planning to watch an NHL game together.（ T / F ）

(3) The Brown Family keeps two pets: a rabbit and a cat.　　　　　　　　　　　　（ T / F ）

(4) Kimura Yumi's host family wants her to show how to cook *nikujaga*.　　　　　（ T / F ）

6【Further Practice】ホストファミリーからのメールを読み，次の問いに英語で答えましょう。

(1) What does their son want to do with Yumi?

　　_____.

(2) What is the host family going to do during her staying?

　　_____.

(3) What kind of animals does the host family have?

　　_____.

(4) What does the host mother want to know?

　　_____.

1 【本文理解】区切りに気をつけて音読し，下の問いに答えましょう。

About 60% / of the human body / consists of water. // When about 2% of water in the
S   V

body / is lost, / it is said / that we feel thirsty / and the exercise capacity gets low. // And, /

when more than 20% is lost, / our life is in danger. // Water is one of the essential things /
S   V   C

for us. // We need to take clean water / into our bodies / constantly / by drinking water /

or eating meals. // We think / that ❶it is something natural. //

But in developing countries, / many people can't obtain clean water / in times of

drought. // They drink dirty water / from rivers or ponds, / and their health is sometimes

damaged. // **G** ❷What they need now / is clean water to drink. //
(関係代名詞)

(1) 下線部❶ it はどのような内容を指すのか，文中の語句で答えましょう。

_____

(2) 下線部❷ What は何を指すのか，文中の語句で答えましょう。

_____

2 【単語】次の語句の意味を調べて書きましょう。

(1) purify(ing) 動(　　　　　　) (2) capacity 名(　　　　　　)
(3) essential 形(　　　　　　) (4) obtain 動(　　　　　　)
(5) drought 名(　　　　　　) (6) powder 名(　　　　　　)

Nice Fit 本文から抜き出しましょう。

運動能力が低下する = (　　　　)(　　　　)(　　　　)(　　　　)(　　　　)

Coffee Break

capacity（お尻につけて形容詞から名詞）
capacity のように，お尻に -ity をつけて形容詞から名詞にするものに下記のようなものがあります。
-ity, -ness

  英会話 footwork   Do you think more people will put solar panels on their houses in the future?

Grammar

関係代名詞 what

関係代名詞の what は，先行詞をとらず〈the thing(s) which 〜〉という意味を表します。

<u>What</u> they need now is clean water to drink. ＝(The thing which)

Some people in the world cannot drink <u>what</u> people usually drink. ＝(the things which)

what は先行詞を含む関係代名詞で，「〜すること [もの]」という意味になるね。

名詞は文の主語・補語・目的語・前置詞の目的語になれるはよね。what の節も同じよ。

3 【文法】日本語に合う英文になるように，（　　）内の語を並べかえましょう。

(1) 私はあなたの言うことが理解できない。　I cannot (what / say / understand / you).

I cannot _____.

(2) 君とって大切なことは私にも大切です。

(important / is / is / you / to / what) also important to me.

_____ also important to me.

(3) 私たちの村は10年前とは違う。

Our village is different (ago / it / ten / was / what / years / from).

Our village is different _____.

(4) 私は彼から聞いたことを信じます。　I (me / believe / he / what / told).

I _____.

4 【表現】日本語に合う英文になるように，　　　　から適切な語を選んで空所に書きましょう。

(1) パスワードは8つ以上の文字で構成されなくてはならない。

Your password should _____ _____ at least 8 characters.

(2) 彼らは自分たちの命が危険にさらされている気がした。

They felt that their lives _____ _____ _____.

| of | in | were | consist | danger |

5 【内容理解】本文の内容に合うように，次の質問に対する適切な答えをア〜エから選びましょう。

Why is the health of many people in developing countries sometimes damaged? (　　　)

ア　Because about 60% of the human body consists of water.

イ　Because they drink dirty water from rivers or ponds.

ウ　Because it is quite possible for them to obtain clean water in time of drought.

エ　Because they think that water is something natural.

1 【本文理解】音声を聞いて，区切りに気をつけて音読し，下の問いに答えましょう。

In the aftermath / of the Great Hanshin Earthquake, / in Hanshin and Awaji, / the water supply was stopped. // Oda Kanetoshi waited / in a long line / in front of water trucks, / then / he saw the water / in a pond nearby / and thought, / "I wish / I could drink the pond water." // Then / he remembered one sentence / of a thesis, / "Poly-glutamic acid / has the potential quality / to purify water, / and ❶it's found / in *natto*." // This statement lit / Oda's soul. // After many trials and errors / for several years, / **G** it was a water-purifying powder / that he finally succeeded / in developing. //
(強調構文)

When you put / one spoonful of water-purifying powder / in water / full of green algae, / ❷they coagulate in a flash. // It precipitates / to the bottom, / and clean water is left. // This purified water / is good to drink. //

(1) 下線部❶ it は何を指すのか，文中の語句で答えましょう。 _____

(2) 下線部❷ they は何を指すのか，文中の語句で答えましょう。 _____

2 【単語】次の語句の意味を調べて書きましょう。

(1)	aftermath	名( )	(2)	supply	名( )
(3)	truck(s)	名( )	(4)	nearby	形( )
(5)	thesis	名( )	(6)	poly-glutamic acid	名( )
(7)	potential	形( )	(8)	statement	名( )
(9)	trial(s)	名( )	(10)	error(s)	名( )
(11)	spoonful	名( )	(12)	algae	名( )
(13)	coagulate	動( )	(14)	precipitate(s)	動( )

Nice Fit 本文から抜き出しましょう。試行錯誤 = ( )( )( )

☕ Coffee Break

coagulate（頭につけていっしょの仲間で，こりかたまる）
coagulate の co- のように，頭につけて「いっしょの，仲間で，こりかたまる」の意味をもつものに，下記のようなものがあります。
con-, syn-, sym-, cor-, col-

英会話 footwork

Do you expect that the number of people who buy things online will increase in the future?

強調構文

〈It is[was] 〜 that …〉の形で，〜に入る語句を強調します。残りの文はそのまま that の後に続ければよい。

It was a water-purifying powder **that** he finally succeeded in developing.

It was in time of the Great Earthquake **that** the water supply was stopped.

〈It is 〜 that …〉で「…するのは〜だ」という意味になるのね。

強調する語句は It is と that の間だよ。

3 【文法】日本語に合う英文になるように，次の英文を 4 通りの強調構文に書きかえましょう。

I sent my brother to her office yesterday.（私は昨日弟を彼女の事務所へやった。）

(1) 昨日弟を彼女の事務所へやったのは，ほかでもない「私」だった。

_____

(2) 私が昨日彼女の事務所へやったのは，ほかでもない「弟」だった。

_____

(3) 私が昨日弟をやったのは，ほかでもない「彼女の事務所へ」であった。

_____

(4) 私が弟を彼女の事務所へやったのは，ほかでもない「昨日」だった。

_____

4 【表現】日本語に合う英文になるように，☐☐☐から適切な語を選んで空所に書きましょう。

(1) 私は欲しい物をうまく手に入れることができた。

I _____ _____ _____ what I wanted.

(2) 紅茶に砂糖をスプーン一杯加えてください。

Please add _____ _____ _____ _____ in my tea.

(3) スカーレットはあっという間に去ってしまった。

Scarlet was gone in a _____.

flash	sugar	of	spoonful	a	getting	in	succeeded

5 【内容理解】本文の内容に合う文は T を，合わない文は F を◯で囲みましょう。

(1) Oda Kanetoshi drank the water in a pond after the great earthquake in 1995. （ T / F ）

(2) One sentence of a thesis says poly-glutamic acid has the potential quality to purify water.

（ T / F ）

(3) It was Oda Kanetoshi that succeeded in developing a water-purifying powder. （ T / F ）

(4) The purified water by poly-glutamic acid is not good to drink. （ T / F ）

Yes. Shopping online is more convenient than going to stores.

1 【本文理解】音声を聞いて，区切りに気をつけて音読し，下の問いに答えましょう。

> **G** Visiting Bangladesh, / Oda was shocked / to see the local people / drink water / from
> (分詞構文)   S   V
> the unimaginably dirty rivers / or use ❶it for cooking. // Since he knew / many infants
> could die of diarrhea / caused by this dirty water, / he thought, / "I would like to offer
> them / good and delicious water. // But if I keep on giving it to them / for free, / my
> company will go bankrupt. // And, / more than anything, / the local people won't be able /
>   S   V   C
> to be independent." // Then, / he sold the purifying powder, / which he developed by
> himself, / for a low price, / in order to offer / precious drinking water / to the people / in
> developing countries / all over the world. // **G** Letting ❷them sell the powder, / ❸he also
>   (分詞構文)
> creates employment / to eliminate poverty. //

(1) 下線部❶ it は何を指すのか，文中の語句で答えましょう。　＿＿＿＿＿＿

(2) 下線部❷ them は誰を指すのか，文中の語句で答えましょう。　＿＿＿＿＿＿

(3) 下線部❸ he は誰を指すのか，文中の語で答えましょう。　＿＿＿＿＿＿

2 【単語】次の語句の意味を調べて書きましょう。

(1) shock(ed)* 　動（　　　　） 　(2) unimaginably 　副（　　　　）

(3) infant(s) 　名（　　　　） 　(4) die of ～* 　（　　　　）

(5) diarrhea 　名（　　　　） 　(6) offer* 　動（　　　　）

(7) bankrupt 　形（　　　　） 　(8) independent 　形（　　　　）

(9) employment 　名（　　　　） 　(10) eliminate 　動（　　　　）

(11) poverty 　名（　　　　）

Nice Fit 本文から抜き出しましょう。

廉価で，安い値段で = (　　　　)(　　　　)(　　　　)(　　　　)

☕ Coffee Break

unimaginably, independent（頭につけてつくる反意語）
unimaginably の un- や independent の in- のように，頭につけて反意語をつくるものに，下記のような
ものがあります。
im-, mis-, dis-, non-

英会話 footwork

Are you afraid that children are easily influenced by violent movies?

分詞構文

動詞の ing 形が文全体や動詞を修飾することがあります。分詞の意味上の主語と文の主語が一致しないものは文法的には誤りとされ、「ずっこけ分詞」（江川泰一郎）と呼ばれています。

時を表す分詞構文（＝When 〜）：「〜する時」「〜する間」という意味を表します。

付帯状況を表す分詞構文（＝While 〜）：「〜ながら」という意味を表します。

<u>Visiting</u> Bangladesh, Oda was shocked to see the local people drink water from the unimaginably dirty rivers or use it for cooking.

<u>Letting</u> them sell the powder, he also creates employment to eliminate poverty.

現在分詞で始まる句は、「〜している時(時)」「〜しながら(付帯状況)」「〜ので(理由)」などの意味を表すよ。

分詞構文は意味の手がかりが少ないので、前後の文脈によって意味を推測してね。

3 【文法】次の各組の 2 文がほぼ同じ意味を表すように、空所に適当な 1 語を入れましょう。

(1) While I was traveling in Okinawa, I saw my old friend.

_____ in Okinawa, I saw my old friend.

(2) As he felt well, he went out for a walk.

_____ well, she went out for a walk.

(3) When she entered the room, she saw a total stranger to her.

_____ the room, she saw a total stranger to her.

(4) When they saw us, they waved their hands.

_____ us, they waved their hands.

4 【表現】日本語に合う英文になるように、◻◻から適当な語を選んで空所に書きましょう。

(1) 我々は挑戦し続けなければならない。

We _____ _____ _____ _____.

(2) 4 歳未満の子供は無料で乗車できます。

Children under four can travel _____ _____.

free	for	must	keep	on	trying

5 【内容理解】本文の内容に合う文は T を、合わない文は F を○で囲みましょう。

(1) Oda was pleased to see the local people in Bangladesh drink water from the dirty rivers.

(T / F)

(2) In Bangladesh, Oda saw the local people use water from the dirty rivers for cooking.

(T / F)

(3) Oda decided to keep on giving good and delicious water to many infants in Bangladesh.

(T / F)

(4) Oda sold the purifying powder, which he developed with ODA, for a low price.　(T / F)

No. Many children know that violence is wrong.

87

Lesson 10 Purifying Powder

1 【本文理解】音声を聞いて，区切りに気をつけて音読し，下の問いに答えましょう。

> As the purifying powder / was becoming increasingly popular / through the sales efforts / of female vendors / known as "Polyglu Ladies," / ordinary families came to buy ❶it. // It is an important source / of additional income / for ❷them. // Polyglu Ladies contribute very much / to the women's economic / and psychological independence. //
>   Oda says, / "I have made many mistakes. // But I can surely assert / that thanks to those mistakes, / I could achieve success / with this project. // I am over sixty years old, / and now I have realized / why I was born. // I can tell you / G how to make your life / useful. // As long as I am fine and energetic, / I want to see people / all over the world / drink clean water. // Now / I feel / I definitely ❸can." //

(1)　下線部❶ it は何を指すのか，文中の語句で答えましょう。　＿＿＿＿＿＿
(2)　下線部❷ them は誰を指すのか，文中の語句で答えましょう。　＿＿＿＿＿＿
(3)　下線部❸ can の後に省略されているものを，文中の語句で答えましょう。　＿＿＿＿＿＿

2 【単語】次の語句の意味を調べて書きましょう。

(1)　increasingly　副（　　　　　　）　(2)　vendor(s)　名（　　　　　　）
(3)　polyglu　名（　　　　　　）　(4)　additional　形（　　　　　　）
(5)　contribute　動（　　　　　　）　(6)　economic　形（　　　　　　）
(7)　psychological　形（　　　　　　）　(8)　assert　動（　　　　　　）
(9)　achieve　動（　　　　　　）　(10)　energetic　形（　　　　　　）
(11)　definitely　副（　　　　　　）

Nice Fit 本文から抜き出しましょう。

女性の経済的・心理的自立 ＝

(　　　　　)(　　　　　)(　　　　　)(　　　　　)(　　　　　)(　　　　　)

Coffee Break

energetic（お尻につけて名詞から形容詞）
energetic の -ic のように，お尻につけて名詞から形容詞にするものに，下記のようなものがあります。
-al, -ous, -y, -ful, -able, -ive, -ible, -ish, -ly

英会話
footwork

Do you assert that the government should make a law to stop people from using smartphones or cell phones while walking?

SVOO (how to ～)

「O に～する方法を V する」という意味になります。

I can tell you <u>how to make</u> your life useful.
S   V   O   O

Polyglu Ladies show people <u>how to contribute</u>
S   V   O   O

to the women's independence.

この文型でよく使われる動詞は, ask, tell, show などだよ。

O（人）には人称代名詞の目的格 (me, him, her) などが入るよ。

3 【文法】日本語に合う英文になるように,（   ）内の語句を並べかえましょう。

(1) ファックスの使い方を教えてください。

Please (how / show / use / me / to) the fax machine.

Please _____ the fax machine.

(2) 座席の予約の仕方を知っていますか。　Do you (reserve / seat / a / to / how / know)?

Do you _____ ?

(3) 諭吉は塾生たちに泳ぎ方を教えた。　Yukichi (swim / taught / to / the students / how).

Yukichi _____ .

(4) 私はあなたの家への行き方を知りません。　I (house / know / to / your / get / how / don't / to).

I _____ .

4 【表現】日本語に合う英文になるように, 空所に適切な語を書きましょう。

(1) グレース・ダーリングは勇敢な少女として知られた。

Grace Darling _____ _____ _____ a brave girl.

(2) 君のおかげで, 時間を全部使ってしまい3時間残業しなければならなかった。

_____ _____ you, I spent all my time and had to work more than three hours overtime.

(3) 晩ご飯までに帰って来るなら出かけてもいいよ。

You can go _____ _____ _____ you're home for dinner.

5 【内容理解】本文の内容に合うように, 次の質問に対する適切な答えをア～エから選びましょう。

Why does Oda think he was born?　　　　　　　　　　　　（　　　）

ア　He was born to make a huge amount of money.

イ　He was born to build a bridge of friendship between Japan and Bangladesh.

ウ　He was born to turn sea water into fresh water.

エ　He was born to see people all over the world drink clean water.

Yes. People using cellphones while walking can cause accidents.

1 【英語定義】次の英語の定義に相当する英単語を書きなさい。 〈5点×5〉

(1) continuous period of dry weather causing distress; want of rain _____

(2) sudden, violent movement of the earth's surface _____

(3) state of being poor _____

(4) helpful; producing good results by helping you to do or achieve what you want _____

(5) look up to _____

2 【ストーリー・リテリング】教科書 p.142（Section 3）を4回音読した後，次の語句をすべて用いて本文を自分の言葉で再現しなさい。 〈10点〉

[使用語句]：Bangladesh, Oda, dirty water, for free, employment

_____

_____

_____

3 【文法】日本語に合う英文になるように，（　　）内の語を並べかえなさい。 〈5点×4〉

(1) 私が初めてその女性に会ったのは，旭川だった。

(woman / the / I / Asahikawa / was / it / in / that / saw) for the first time.

_____ for the first time.

(2) 君に必要なのは十分な睡眠だ。 (is / need / you / good / what / a) sleep.

_____ sleep.

(3) カフェテリアに入ると，友人の一人がロコモコを食べているのが見えた。

(eating / entering / , / friend / saw / a / I / the cafeteria / mine / of) loco moco.

_____ loco moco.

(4) 私が彼に泳ぎ方を教えた。 (him / swim / to / how / taught / I).

_____ .

4 【文法】日本語に合う英文になるように，空所に適切な語を書きなさい。 〈6点×3〉

(1) 彼はマルタに来て初めて英語を話すことを楽しむことができた。

_____ was not _____ he came to Malta _____ he could enjoy speaking English.

(2) 日本人はよく私に英語を話せるようになる方法は何かと聞いてくる。

Japanese often ask me _____ _____ _____ _____ .

(3) バンクーバー（Vancouver）に滞在中に，私はこれらのコインを収集した。

_____ _____ _____ , I collected these coins.

5 【内容理解】次の英文を読んで，下の問いに答えなさい。 〈計27点〉

In the aftermath of the Great Hanshin Earthquake, in Hanshin and Awaji, the water supply was stopped. Oda Kanetoshi waited in a long line in front of water trucks, then he saw the water in a pond nearby and thought, "I wish I could drink the pond water." Then he remembered one sentence of a thesis, "Poly-glutamic acid has the potential quality to purify water, and it's found in *natto*." This statement lit Oda's soul. After many trials and errors for several years, ①he finally succeeded in developing a water-purifying powder.

When you put one spoonful of water-purifying powder in water full of green algae, they coagulate in a flash. It precipitates to the bottom, and clean water is left. This purified water is good to drink.

②When Oda visited Bangladesh, he was shocked to see the local people drink water from the unimaginably dirty rivers or use it for cooking. Since he knew many infants could die of diarrhea caused by this dirty water, he thought, "I would like to offer them good and delicious water. But if I keep on giving it to them for free, my company will go bankrupt. And, more than anything, the local people won't be able to be independent." Then, he sold the purifying powder, which he developed by himself, for a low price, in order to offer precious drinking water to the people in developing countries all over the world. ③While he lets them sell the powder, he also creates employment to eliminate poverty.

(1) 下線部①を強調構文を用いて，下線部②と③を分詞構文を用いて書きかえなさい。 (9点×3)

① …＿＿＿＿＿＿＿＿＿＿＿＿＿＿＿＿＿＿＿＿＿＿＿＿＿＿＿＿＿＿＿＿＿ .

② ＿＿＿＿＿＿＿＿＿＿＿＿＿＿＿＿＿＿＿＿＿＿＿＿＿＿＿＿＿＿＿＿＿＿

＿＿＿＿＿＿＿＿＿＿＿＿＿＿＿＿＿＿＿＿＿＿＿＿＿＿＿＿＿＿＿＿＿＿ .

③ ＿＿＿＿＿＿＿＿＿＿＿＿＿＿＿＿＿＿＿＿＿＿＿＿＿＿＿＿＿＿＿＿＿＿ .

【1】　次の各組の文の文型を指摘して，和訳しましょう。

(1)　Anne made a pretty doll.

　　　第_____文型　_____

(2)　Anne made him a new cap.

　　　第_____文型　_____

(3)　Anne made him happy.

　　　第_____文型　_____

(4)　Gordon found the book easily.

　　　第_____文型　_____

(5)　Gordon found the book easy.

　　　第_____文型　_____

【2】　次の文中の誤りを正しましょう。

(1)　Stay here till the lights will turn green.

　　　→　_____

(2)　I can't go on vacation because I broke my leg.

　　　→　_____

(3)　She lost the hat that I gave her as a Christmas gift.

　　　→　_____

(4)　I am belonging to the futsal club.

　　　→　_____

(5)　I have just gone to the station to see my cousin off.

　　　→　_____

【3】　次の各組の文がほぼ同じ意味を表すように，(　　)内に適当な語を入れましょう。

(1)　It was not necessary for him to go, but he went.

　　　= He (　　　　　　) (　　　　　　　　) have gone.

(2)　He doesn't have the courage to make a speech.

　　　= He (　　　　　　) (　　　　　　　　) make a speech.

(3)　We should be kind to the old. = We (　　　　　　) (　　　　　　　　) be kind to the old.

(4)　I ordered them to clean the room.

　　　= I ordered that (　　　　　　　) (　　　　　　　) clean the room.

(5)　He was in the habit of sitting for hours reading.

　　　= He (　　　　　　) (　　　　　　　　) sit for hours reading.

助動詞 ・ 受け身

▶pp.166-171

【4】 次の各文を受け身にかえましょう。

(1) The doctor closed the door.

_____

(2) Do they speak French in Canada?

_____

(3) Jane did not help Daddy.

_____

(4) The dog has killed a bird.

_____

(5) They are building a new covered bridge over the river.

_____

【5】 次の文を英語で書きましょう。

(1) キララは台所で母親の手伝いをしています。

_____

(2) 彼らはドアを空けはなしにしておいた。

_____

(3) 良夫はよく先生にほめられる。

_____

(4) 彼女はそんなことをする必要はなかったのに。

_____

(5) コロナ（COVID-19）は間もなく撲滅（eradicate）されるだろう。

_____

【1】　（　　）内の指示に従って，次の文を書きかえましょう。

(1) Lake Biwa is the largest lake in Japan.　（比較級を用いて）

_____

(2) Dunk is the tallest girl in our school.　（原級を用いて）

_____

(3) This book is not as difficult as that.　（less を用いて）

_____

(4) He is cleverer than any other boy in our class.　（最上級を用いて）

_____

(5) This is the most amusing story I have ever read.　（原級を用いて）

_____

【2】　次の文中の誤りを正して，全文を書きましょう。

(1) Did you hear her to sing?

_____

(2) He was seen cross the street.

_____

(3) You had not better to go out in such a rain.

_____

(4) I must get him copy this report.

_____

(5) I will have him to carry the baggage upstairs.

_____

【3】　次の各文の下線部を，分詞を用いて書きかえましょう。

(1) Look at the girl who is dancing.

_____

(2) She lent me a book which was written in German.

_____

(3) The goods that were ordered last month have not yet arrived.

_____

(4) The tree that stands near the gate has lovely flowers.

_____

(5) A dog that are barking seldom bites.

_____

知覚　・　使役

▶pp.172-173

【4】　分詞構文を用いて，次の文を書きかえましょう。

(1)　When she saw her son, she shouted with joy.

_____

(2)　Because I did not feel well, I stayed at home all day.

_____

(3)　Because I had finished my work, I had nothing to do.

_____

(4)　It was a very dull meeting, so I left as soon as I could.

_____

(5)　If we judge from his accent, he must be an Australian.

_____

【5】　次の文を英語で書きましょう。

(1)　彼は彼女ほどの身長はない。

_____

(2)　富士山は日本でいちばん高い山である。

_____

(3)　正午に鐘が鳴るのが毎日聞こえます。

_____

(4)　私は友だちに写真をとってもらった。

_____

(5)　空模様(the look of the sky)から見れば，午後は雪だろう。

_____

文法のまとめ　　動名詞　・　不定詞

【1】　次の各文を日本語に直し，それぞれの不定詞の用法を説明しましょう。

(1)　To see you is always a great pleasure.

_____　[　　　]　的用法

(2)　Give me something cold to drink.

_____　[　　　]　的用法

(3)　She went to Italy to study music.

_____　[　　　]　的用法

(4)　I was very surprised to hear the news.

_____　[　　　]　的用法

(5)　Pierre Cardin lived to be ninety-eight.

_____　[　　　]　的用法

【2】　次の語を並べかえて，意味の通る文にしましょう。

(1)　Bible, through, the, difficult, it, found, to I, read.

_____

(2)　you, do, all, to, have, best, to, is, your, do.

_____

(3)　build, yet, where, you, have, house, to your, decided?

_____

(4)　the, seen, to, star, sky, in, be, was, a, not.

_____

(5)　way, me, to, kind, she, the, show, enough, was.

_____

【3】　次の(　　)の中に適当な語を入れ，全文を和訳しましょう。

(1)　I cannot (　　　　　　) laughing at his yellow tie.

_____

(2)　She didn't feel (　　　　　　) going out that evening.

_____

(3)　It is (　　　　　　) use my arguing with you.

_____

(4)　It goes (　　　　　　) saying that health is more precious than wealth.

_____

(5)　Illness (　　　　　　) me from attending the party yesterday.

_____

【4】 次の文中の下線部の誤りを正しましょう。

(1) Would you mind <u>to lend</u> me some money?

_____

(2) He has just finished <u>to read</u> *War and Peace* by Tolstoy.

_____

(3) It is difficult to give up <u>to smoke</u> in a day.

_____

(4) Remember <u>mailing</u> the letter on your way to school.

_____

(5) I am looking forward to <u>see</u> you soon.

_____

【5】 次の文を英語で書きましょう。

(1) 本当のことを言うと，私は犬が好きではありません。

_____

(2) このお茶は熱すぎて飲めない。

_____

(3) 今夜は数学(math)を勉強する気がしない。

_____

(4) この記事(article)は読む価値がないと思います。

_____

(5) 君はそんなことを言ったのを恥じていないのか。

_____

【1】　次の文を仮定法に書きかえましょう。

(1)　As Taka is in bad health, he can't study hard.

_____

(2)　I am sorry that you are not here.

_____

(3)　As you got angry, she went out of the room.

_____

(4)　Because he was busy, he could not go there.

_____

(5)　It rained last night, so the road is bad now.

_____

【2】　細部に注意して，次の文の意味を日本語で書きましょう。

(1)　If he is honest, I will employ him.

_____

(2)　If he were honest, I would employ him.

_____

(3)　I'll tell him so when he comes here.

_____

(4)　I don't know when he will come here.

_____

(5)　I don't know if it will rain tomorrow, but if it rains, I will stay at home.

_____

【3】　次の各組の文を，関係代名詞を用いて一つの文にまとめましょう。

(1)　Hyuma is the boy. + His father is a professional baseball player.

_____

(2)　The man is my uncle. + He is reading a newspaper.

_____

(3)　A planet is a star. + It moves around the sun.

_____

(4)　I bought this dictionary. + And, it helped me a lot.

_____

(5)　Mitsuru has a new car. + He is very proud of it.

_____

条件節 ・ 仮定法

▶pp.176-179

【4】 次の各組の文を，関係副詞を用いて一つの文にまとめましょう。

(1) This is the place ＋ I lost my digital single-lens reflex camera here.

_____

(2) I went over the garden. ＋ And, there she was sitting under a tree.

_____

(3) Why did the lights go out? ＋ Nobody knew the reason.

_____

(4) The time will come. ＋ Your dream will come true then.

_____

(5) We wash our faces out of doors like this. ＋ This is the way.

_____

【5】 次の文を英語で書きましょう。

(1) もう５分早く来たら，あなたはバスに間に合ったのに。

_____

(2) 彼女は，まるで男の子のようにふるまう(behave)。

_____

(3) もし彼が来れば，一緒にコンサートに行こう。

_____

(4) 利子(としこ)には，銀行に勤めているおじがいます。

_____

(5) 火曜日は，彼がたいへん忙しい日です。

_____

総合問題 1

1 右上の QR コードまたは CD の音声を聞き，次の問い（A，B）に答えなさい。

A それぞれの問いについて対話を聞き，答えとして最も適切なものを，ア〜エから選んで答えなさい。

(1) When does the wheelchair basketball game start?　CD6 11

ア　At 3:00.　　　イ　At 3:30.　　　ウ　At 4:00.　　　エ　At 4:30.

（　　　）

(2) Why didn't Mark do well on the Japanese history test?　CD6 12

ア　He didn't know there was a test.

イ　It was more difficult than he thought.

ウ　He couldn't study much for the test.

エ　Japanese history isn't his favorite subject.

（　　　）

B これから流れる英語を聞いて，それぞれの問いの答えとして最も適切なものをア〜エから選んで答えなさい。CD6 13

(1) What did Patty's picture postcard look like?　　　　　　　　　　（　　　）

ア　　　　　　　　　　　　　　　　　　　　ウ　　　　　　　エ

(2) Which season is Yasuko enjoying now?

ア　Spring.　　　イ　Summer.　　　ウ　Fall.　　　エ　Winter.

（　　　）

(3) Why was Mary surprised?

ア　She got the letters at the same time.

イ　It is very cold in Japan.

ウ　Her letter did not arrive.

エ　Her friends were living in different seasons.

（　　　）

2 次の各文の（　　）内に入る最も適当なものをそれぞれ 1 つ選び，記号で答えなさい。

(1) Mr. Smith is (　　) teacher. He is very kind.

ア　we　　　　イ　our　　　　ウ　us　　　　エ　ours

(2) (　　) careful when you cross the street.

ア　Am　　　　イ　Are　　　　ウ　Is　　　　エ　Be

(3) I (　　　) in Yokohama for three years.

    ア　was lived　　　　　イ　have lived　　　　ウ　living　　　　　エ　lives

(4) (　　　) you tell me more about the person?

    ア　Shall　　　　　　イ　May　　　　　　　ウ　Will　　　　　　エ　Have

(5) Mike (　　　) a walk before breakfast every day.

    ア　gives　　　　　　イ　makes　　　　　　ウ　looks　　　　　　エ　takes

(6) A (　　　) tells us what is happening in the world.

    ア　newspaper　　　　イ　mail　　　　　　ウ　test　　　　　　エ　diary

(7) She has gained weight, (　　　) she will go on a diet.

    ア　because　　　　　イ　so　　　　　　　ウ　or　　　　　　　エ　if

(8) "What do you want for your birthday present?" "I want a (　　　) of jogging shoes."

    ア　piece　　　　　　イ　gram　　　　　　ウ　pair　　　　　　エ　sheet

(9) "What are you doing here?" "We are looking (　　　) our lost bags."

    ア　with　　　　　　　イ　on　　　　　　　ウ　for　　　　　　　エ　under

(10) "(　　　) did you pay for the dress?" "About 30,000 yen."

    ア　How much　　　　イ　How many　　　　ウ　How often　　　　エ　How far

[3] 次の各日本文の意味を表すように，(　　　)内の語句を並べかえて正しい英文を作るとき，(　　　)内で5番目に来るものをそれぞれ1つ選び，記号で答えなさい。

(1) 生徒たちは，浦安行きのバスを待っている。

    The students (the bus / to / for / which / are / goes / waiting) Urayasu.

    ア　the bus　　　　　イ　for　　　　　　　ウ　which　　　　　エ　waiting

(2) 私が小樽駅に着いたとき，たくさん雪が降っていた。

    It (snowing / I / when / was / at / a lot / arrived) Otaru Station.

    ア　I　　　　　　　　イ　when　　　　　　ウ　at　　　　　　　エ　a lot

(3) 生徒たちは先生の話を注意深く聞いている。

    (their / are / to / teacher / the / listening / students) carefully.

    ア　their　　　　　　イ　to　　　　　　　ウ　the　　　　　　エ　listening

(4) 少しの間，電子辞書を貸していただけませんか。

    Please (your / me / dictionary / a while / lend / electronic / for).

    ア　your　　　　　　イ　me　　　　　　　ウ　dictionary　　　エ　for

(5) この電車は何時に出発するか知っていますか。

    (this train / know / will / what / you / do / time) leave?

    ア　know　　　　　　イ　will　　　　　　ウ　what　　　　　エ　time

(6) ケンはナンシーほど多くの本を持っていない。

    Ken (have / Nancy / books / as / as / doesn't / many).

    ア　have　　　　　　イ　books　　　　　ウ　as　　　　　　　エ　many

4 次の各日本文の意味を表すように，（　　　）内に適当な語を入れなさい。

(1) 祖母は私に先週の木曜日プレゼントを買ってくれた。

My (　　　　　) (　　　　　　　　) me a present last (　　　　　　).

(2) このコーヒーは私には熱すぎて飲めない。

This coffee is (　　　　　) hot (　　　　　) me (　　　　　) drink.

(3) あなたは今までに彼の小説を読んだことがありますか。

(　　　　　) you (　　　　　) (　　　　　　) his novels?

(4) 私たちはその女性が路上でけがをしているのを見つけた。

We (　　　　　) the woman (　　　　　　) in the street.

(5) 祖父はぼくを秀一（しゅういち）と名付けたので，みんなぼくのことを秀（しゅう）ちゃんと呼ぶ。

My grandfather (　　　　　) (　　　　　) Shu-ichi, so everyone (　　　　　　　)
(　　　　　) Shu-chan.

(6) 父が帰宅したとき，私は宿題をしていた。

I (　　　　　) (　　　　　　) my homework when my father came home.

(7) 私はヤスコに何年も会っていない。

I (　　　　　) (　　　　　) Yasuko (　　　　　) many years.

(8) 私は簡単にその英語の本を見つけた。

I (　　　　　) the English book (　　　　　).

(9) 彼は彼女にダイヤの指輪を買ってあげた。

He (　　　　　) a diamond ring (　　　　　) (　　　　　).

(10) 「ロメオとジュリエット」はシェークスピアが書いた劇だ。

Romeo and Juliet is a play (　　　　　) (　　　　　) Shakespeare.

5 次の対話文を読んで，あとの問いに答えなさい。

Peter: What are your plans for the future, Kikue?

Kikue: I want to learn cooking and become a cook.

Peter: Why?

Kikue: Because I love cooking. I often cook for my family. Cooking *udon* is fun. Hamburgers are good, but I like Japanese food better. Do you like Japanese food?

Peter: (　①　) I like *tofu* more than anything else. I sometimes eat *tempura* and *sukiyaki*.

Kikue: I'm glad to hear that. I've heard *sushi* is becoming more popular in some foreign countries.

Peter: That is right.

Kikue: I want to be a cook and work in a foreign country some day.

Peter: Then I will visit you.

Kikue: (　②　) Please come and see me.

Peter: Which country do you want to live in after you become a cook?

Kikue: Well, I think America is a nice country to live in.

Peter: How about my country, Australia?

Kikue: I want to go there, but I want to live in America.

Peter: Why?

Kikue: Because I want to be a cook in a big city.

Peter: There are big cities in Australia.

Kikue: I mean a big city like New York.

Peter: (③)

Kikue: I know Sydney is a big city in Australia. But New York is a big city in the world.

(1) （ ① ）〜（ ③ ）に入る最も適当なものをそれぞれ１つ選び，記号で答えなさい。

ア　Do you have any ideas?　　　　イ　I see.

ウ　Yes, I do.　　　　　　　　　　エ　No, I don't.

オ　Who knows?　　　　　　　　　カ　I hope so.

(2) 本文の内容に合うように（ ⓐ ），（ ⓑ ）にそれぞれ適当な日本語を入れなさい。

> 菊枝の知り合いであるピーターは（ ⓐ ）出身である。彼は日本食の中でも，特に（ ⓑ ）が好きである。

(3) 本文の内容に一致するものを１つ選び，記号で答えなさい。

ア　Kikue wants to learn cooking because Peter loves cooking.

イ　Kikue cooked Japanese food for Peter but he didn't like it.

ウ　Kikue doesn't want to go to Australia because she has been there before.

エ　Kikue wants to live in America after becoming a cook.

6 次の文を読んで，あとの問いに答えなさい。

I'm Luna Brown. I first joined the dance club when I was 10. I liked it very much. But last year, when I was 14, I stopped enjoying dancing because I realized I was not so good.

When there was a solo part in a performance, our teacher always chose a girl called Mia. Mia was a very good dancer. When Mia danced, everyone got excited and watched her dance. After a performance, people were always saying to Mia, "You danced so well. You are so talented." I wanted people to say ①this to me, too. I practiced every day. I practiced very hard. Soon, I stopped dancing with other teammates and only took care of my own dance. I started to hate joint practice, and I didn't like Mia very much, either. She never practiced hard, but she always did well.

One day, my teacher, Mrs. Wilson, said she wanted to talk to me. She asked me, "Is something wrong, Luna?" She told me that before I was one of her most enthusiastic students, but now I never smiled, and my dance was getting worse. She felt that I was worried about something.

I said to Mrs. Wilson, "I was practicing so hard. But I will never become as good as Mia." Mrs. Wilson asked me, "Will you be satisfied if you become a better dancer than Mia?" "Yes!" I said without thinking. "Because she is the best?" Mrs. Wilson asked. "Yes!" I said. Mrs. Wilson smiled and said to me, "There are many dancers who are much better than Mia, but it is impossible to choose the 'best' dancer. There will always be someone better. So what does being number one really mean?" "But everyone thinks Mia is the best dancer," I said. Mrs. Wilson then said, "Did you join this dance club and practice only to become number one? Didn't you enjoy dancing?"

Then I realized that Mrs. Wilson was right. I was worried only about other people's opinions. Now I remembered an important thing: dancing with my teammates made me happy and I loved dancing.

②After that day, I practiced hard and did my best, but only *my* best, and not someone else's.

(注)solo：一人の　　joint：合同の　　enthusiastic：熱心な　　satisfied：満足した　　impossible：不可能な

(1) 下線部①の指す内容として最も適当なものを1つ選び，記号で答えなさい。

　　ア　ルナはもっとダンスの練習をすべきということ

　　イ　ルナはプロのダンサーになるべきだということ

　　ウ　ルナにはダンスの才能があるということ

　　エ　ルナにはダンスのアレンジが必要ということ

(2) 本文の内容と合うように次の各文を完成させるとき，（　　）に当てはまる最も適当なものをそれぞれ1つ選び，記号で答えなさい。

A　When she first joined the dance club, Luna (　　　　).

　　ア　was 10 years old and loved dancing

　　イ　was the best dancer of the club

　　ウ　was a junior high schoool student

　　エ　hated dance practice

B　Last year, Luna knew that (　　　　) and stopped enjoying dancing.

　　ア　she couldn't dance in the performance

　　イ　she was a better dancer than Mia

　　ウ　she was not so good at dancing

　　エ　she didn't have to practice so hard

C　Luna didn't like Mia very much, because (　　　　).

　　ア　Mia danced as well as Luna

　　イ　Mia never practiced hard, but she was a very good dancer

　　ウ　Mia practiced the hardest in the club

　　エ　Mia loved dance as much as Luna

(3) 以下の文は下線部②の理由をまとめたものである。（　ⓐ　）〜（　ⓒ　）にそれぞれ適当な日本語を入れなさい。

> 今までは（　ⓐ　）の意見ばかりを気にしていたが，ウィルソン先生から，大切なのは（　ⓑ　）になることではなく，ダンスを（　ⓒ　）ことであると学んだから。

(4) 本文の内容に一致するものを1つ選び，記号で答えなさい。
- ア　Luna was chosen a solo dancer in the performance by her teacher.
- イ　Luna thought Ms. Wilson was wrong and didn't like her.
- ウ　Luna remembered she loved dancing, and started to do her best.
- エ　Luna wanted to make more friends in the club, but she couldn't.

7 次の文を読んで，あとの問いに答えなさい。

Do you like the sea? I think many people like the sea and have had a lot of chances to swim there. But what do you know about the sea? For example, which is longer, the height of the highest mountain on land or the depth of the deepest sea? Which has more kinds of living things, the land or the sea? These questions are not easy, I think. Let's think about these questions about the sea and know more about it.

Before these questions, think about another one. Which is larger, the land or the sea? This question may be (　①　). You can answer the question if you remember a map showing the whole world. About 70% of the earth is the sea. Surveys show that the deepest area in the sea is more than 10,000 meters and this is longer than the height of the highest mountain on land. So the sea is (　②　) than the land.

The first living thing on earth was born in the sea. After that, living things were only in the sea for a very, very long time. Living things in the sea evolved very slowly for a long time. So the sea has a long (　③　) of living things. Also as I told you, the sea is very large and very deep. So the sea also has a lot of space for living things. We only know about a small (　④　) of the sea. And ⑤we can't say how many living things are in the sea. But some people say there are about 10,000,000 kinds of living things in the sea. On land there are about 1,000,000 kinds of living things. More than 90% of all kinds of living things on earth live in the sea. The sea has many kinds of living things.

There is a lot of water on earth. And there are also a lot of living things on earth. So earth is called the planet of water or the planet of living things. We haven't found other planets which have a lot of water or living things. About 98% of the water on earth is in the sea. If we know more about the sea, we can understand our earth and the living things on it better.

（注）height：高さ　　land：陸　　depth：深さ　　survey：調査　　evolve：進化する

(1) （　①　）に入る最も適当なものを1つ選び，記号で答えなさい。
- ア　difficult
- イ　easy
- ウ　good
- エ　bad

(2) （ **②** ）に入る最も適当なものを１つ選び，記号で答えなさい。

　　ア　larger but shorter　　　　　　　　イ　smaller but deeper

　　ウ　smaller and shorter　　　　　　　エ　larger and deeper

(3) （ **③** ），（ **④** ）に入る最も適当なものをそれぞれ１つ選び，記号で答えなさい。

　　ア　fish　　　　　　イ　history　　　　　ウ　science　　　　　エ　river

　　オ　part　　　　　　カ　question

(4) 下線部⑤を日本語に直しなさい。

(5) 本文の内容に一致するものを２つ選び，記号で答えなさい。

　　ア　Many people don't like the sea because they don't know much about it.

　　イ　Surveys show that the height of the highest mountain on land is longer than the depth of the deepest area in the sea.

　　ウ　On earth, the first living thing was born in the sea a long time ago.

　　エ　There is a lot of space for living things in the sea.

　　オ　The land has more than 90% of all kinds of living things on earth.

106

1 右上の QR コードまたは CD の音声を聞き，次の問い（A，B）に答えなさい。

A. それぞれの問いについて対話を聞き，答えとして最も適切なものを，ア～エから選んで答えなさい。

(1) What does the woman advise the man to do?　CD6 14

　ア　Walk to the museum.

　イ　Take a bus.

　ウ　Call a taxi.

　エ　Visit the museum on another day.　　　　　　　　　　　　　　（　　　）

(2) What is the girl's problem?　CD6 15

　ア　Her shoes do not fit her.

　イ　Her broken leg hurts.

　ウ　She is not interested in plants.

　エ　She is not good at running.　　　　　　　　　　　　　　　　　（　　　）

B. これから流れる英語を聞いて，それぞれの問いの答えとして最も適切なものをア～エから選んで答えなさい。CD6 16

(1) Which picture shows Jeff's workplace?　　　　　　　　　　　　　（　　　）

　　　ア　　　　　　　　　イ　　　　　　　　　ウ　　　　　　　　　エ

(2) What did Carolyn suggest to Jeff?

　ア　She suggested he try aromatherapy.

　イ　She suggested he quit the job.

　ウ　She suggested he try dog therapy.

　エ　She suggested he change his job.　　　　　　　　　　　　　　　（　　　）

(3) What will Jeff do this weekend?

　ア　Go to a therapy center.

　イ　Watch a dog race.

　ウ　Study aromatherapy.

　エ　Ask his co-worker for advice.　　　　　　　　　　　　　　　　（　　　）

2 次の各文の（　　）内に入る最も適当なものをそれぞれ１つ選び，記号で答えなさい。

(1) I'm going to give (　　　) a watch.

ア　she　　　　　　イ　her　　　　　　ウ　hers　　　　　　エ　herself

(2) He (　　) absent from school yesterday.

ア　be　　　　　　イ　is　　　　　　ウ　was　　　　　　エ　were

(3) "(　　) this bus go to Utsunomiya?" "No. It goes to Nagoya."

ア　Do　　　　　　イ　Does　　　　　　ウ　Is　　　　　　エ　Are

(4) I have a lot of work (　　) today.

ア　do　　　　　　イ　does　　　　　　ウ　doing　　　　　　エ　to do

(5) Please show me (　　) to cook this fish.

ア　who　　　　　　イ　what　　　　　　ウ　that　　　　　　エ　how

(6) They are proud (　　) their son.

ア　of　　　　　　イ　over　　　　　　ウ　with　　　　　　エ　at

(7) I'll (　　) my best to pass the test.

ア　do　　　　　　イ　tell　　　　　　ウ　study　　　　　　エ　play

(8) Kumi always (　　) off at this bus stop.

ア　puts　　　　　　イ　leaves　　　　　　ウ　takes　　　　　　エ　gets

(9) "There is a lot of (　　) in this park." "Yes. There are cans and bottles everywhere."

ア　air　　　　　　イ　future　　　　　　ウ　garbage　　　　　　エ　life

(10) "Shall I help you with your work?" "(　　)."

ア　No, I won't　　　イ　Yes, please　　　ウ　Yes, I shall　　　エ　No, I shall not

3 次の各日本文の意味を表すように，（　　）内の語句を並べかえて正しい英文を作るとき，（　　）内で５番目に来るものをそれぞれ１つ選び，記号で答えなさい。

(1) ジョンと私はその知らせを聞いてとても悲しかったです。

John (to / were / hear / sad / I / very / and) the news.

ア　to　　　　　　イ　hear　　　　　　ウ　sad　　　　　　エ　very

(2) その母は子どもに，漫画を読むのをやめるよう言いました。

The mother (child / reading / her / stop / told / to / comic books).

ア　child　　　　　　イ　reading　　　　　　ウ　stop　　　　　　エ　to

(3) 私は弟より10センチメートル背が高いです。

(little brother / than / am / taller / I / my / 10 centimeters).

ア　than　　　　　　イ　taller　　　　　　ウ　my　　　　　　エ　10 centimeters

(4) ドアのところに立っている男性を知っていますか。

(the man / you / do / standing / the door / know / at)?

ア　the man　　　　　イ　you　　　　　　ウ　standing　　　　　エ　the door

(5) 海外に何回行ったことがありますか。

(times / how / you / have / abroad / many / been)?

ア　times　　　　　　　イ　you　　　　　　　ウ　many　　　　　　　エ　been

(6) 英語は世界中で話されている言語です。

English (which / a language / is / over / is / all / spoken) the world.

ア　which　　　　　　　イ　a language　　　　ウ　all　　　　　　　エ　spoken

4 次の各日本文の意味を表すように，（　　）内に適当な語を入れなさい。

(1) 私は今年の4月，京都に住んでいる友人に荷物を送った。

I (　　　　　　) a package to my friend (　　　　　　) in Kyoto this (　　　　　　).

(2) 私のいとこは水泳が上手だ。

My (　　　　　) is a (　　　　　) (　　　　　).

(3) ハンスは久幸と同じ年だ。

Hans is (　　　　　) (　　　　　) (　　　　　) Hisayuki.

(4) 私は15題の問題を解かなければならなかったのだが，10題しか解けなかった。

I (　　　　　) (　　　　　) solve 15 problems, but I (　　　　　) (　　　　　) only 10 problems.

(5) すみませんが，コーラをコップ1杯いただけますか。

Excuse me, but (　　　　　) (　　　　　) give me a glass of Coke?

(6) ジョージは半年ほどで日本語を話せるようになるでしょう。

George (　　　　　) be (　　　　　) to speak Japanese (　　　　　) about half a year.

(7) 今日は一昨日より暑い。

It's (　　　　　) today (　　　　　) the day before yesterday.

(8) たとえ明日雪が降っても，私は出かけるつもりです。

I'll go out even (　　　　　) it (　　　　　) snowy tomorrow.

(9) あと10分あれば，私はこの記事を読み終わることができるのに。

(　　　　　) I (　　　　　) 10 minutes more, I (　　　　　) (　　　　　) reading this article.

(10) 上手にスペイン語が話せたらなあ。

I (　　　　　) I (　　　　　) (　　　　　) Spanish well.

5 次の対話文を読んで，あとの問いに答えなさい。

Kentaro: Hi, Mr. Doe. (　①　)

Mr. Doe: Oh, hi, Kentaro. I'm reading a bus timetable. I'm thinking about a bus trip from LosAngeles to New York.

Kentaro: That's nice! (　②　)

Mr. Doe: In the summer vacation.

Kentaro: Great! But I think a bus trip takes long time.

Mr. Doe: Yes. It takes three days if I go there directly.

Kentaro: I see. Going by plane is faster.

Mr. Doe: Yes. That's true. (　③　)

Kentaro: What are they?

Mr. Doe: On the way to New York, I can make stopovers and visit different places. (　④　)

Kentaro: That is interesting. Where will you visit on the way?

Mr. Doe: Look at this map. I will visit Denver and Chicago.

Kentaro: Do you often go there?

Mr. Doe: No. This is my first trip there.

　（注）make stopovers：途中下車する

(1)　（　①　）～（　④　）に入る最も適当なものをそれぞれ1つ選び，記号で答えなさい。

　　ア　But there are some good things about a bus trip.

　　イ　But I hope to make the trips short.

　　ウ　Meeting people in different cities is also fun.

　　エ　Getting there by bus is hard in the summer.

　　オ　What are you doing, sir?

　　カ　Plane trips are better than bus trips.

　　キ　When will you take the trip?

(2)　本文の内容に合うように（　ⓐ　），（　ⓑ　）にそれぞれ適当な日本語を入れなさい。

> 　ドウ先生はこの夏，ロサンゼルスから（　ⓐ　）までのバス旅行を計画している。途中下車してデンバーと（　ⓑ　）に立ち寄る予定である。

(3)　本文の内容に一致するものを1つ選び，記号で答えなさい。

　　ア　If you go from Los Angeles to New York directly by bus, it takes six days.

　　イ　Mr. Doe is thinking about a train trip from Los Angeles to New York.

　　ウ　Los Angeles is just between Denver and New York.

　　エ　Mr. Doe has never been to Denver or Chicago.

6 これは，佑太(Yuta)が書いたスピーチの原稿です。これを読んで，以下の問いに答えなさい。

　I went to London during this summer vacation with my family. This was my first trip to a foreign country, so I was looking forward to it. I wanted to know about London, so I searched for information about it on the Internet. I was able to see many famous things before the trip.

　In London, we went to some popular places. I already saw them on the Internet, but they looked bigger and more beautiful to me (　①　) I saw them directly. I was moved! Then, we went to a restaurant to eat local dishes. They were very new to me, but I enjoyed them. When we finished our dinner and left the restaurant at about nine in the evening, I found one strange thing. It was not dark outside! In Fukushima, it is dark at nine in July, but it is not in London! This was the most interesting thing to me. I enjoyed the trip very much (②) I was able to discover new things.

After the summer vacation, I told my classmates about my trip to London in an English class. Many of them liked my story. After school, one of my classmates came to me and said, "I really enjoyed your story. I love Harry Potter, and I am very interested in London. Can you tell me more about your trip?" In fact, ③I was surprised when she came to talk to me. Before that, we didn't talk, and I thought she was not interested in foreign countries. But she knew a lot about London. We talked about my trip and Harry Potter. I discovered new things about her on that day.

You can get information about many things on TV and the Internet, and you often think you know about people around you before talking to them. But you can discover new things when you experience something directly. I want to remember ④this idea and experience a lot of things in the future.

(注) be moved：感動している　　local dishes：その土地の料理

(1) (①)，(②)に入る最も適当なものをそれぞれ１つずつ選び，記号で答えなさい。

　　ア　if　　　　　　　イ　but　　　　　　　ウ　when　　　　　　エ　because

(2) 佑太がロンドンで１番おもしろいと思ったことを１つ選び，記号で答えなさい。

　　ア　夜９時でも外が暗くなかったこと。

　　イ　有名な場所が予想より大きかったこと。

　　ウ　外国の人と英語で話すことが出来たこと。

　　エ　ロンドンでハリーポッターを見たこと。

(3) 下線部③の理由として適当なものを１つ選び，記号で答えなさい。

　　ア　One of Yuta's classmates asked him about his trip, but he did not talk to her before.

　　イ　One of Yuta's classmates liked his story very much because she went to London before.

　　ウ　One of Yuta's classmates did not talk to him, and she was not interested in foreign countries.

　　エ　One of Yuta's classmates was encouraged by his story, but she could not ask him about London.

(4) 下線部④の内容に合うように(ⓐ)，(ⓑ)にそれぞれ適当な日本語を入れなさい。

> 何かを直接(ⓐ)するときに，新しいことを(ⓑ)することができるという考え。

(5) 本文の内容に一致するものを 1 つ選び，記号で答えなさい。

　ア　Yuta told his family about his trip to London.

　イ　Yuta saw many things about London on the Internet before the trip.

　ウ　Yuta went on a trip to another foreign country after his trip to London.

　エ　Yuta and his family did not think that local foods in London were good.

[7] これは，社会人のスティーブが15歳の頃を思い出して書いたものです。これを読んで，以下の問い
に答えなさい。

When I was fifteen, I was always thinking about my future. I was interested in a lot of jobs, but ①I didn't know which job was the best for me. Then my sister gave me a good idea. It was to visit some of her friends to learn about their jobs.

First, I went to a nice office of a trading company and talked with one of my sister's friends. He said, "I am working with foreign people by using e-mails." He told me about the world, and his story made me very excited.

The next day I met a young doctor in a hospital. ②He looked tired because he came there after he was working all night. He said, "I have a lot of work, but I always do my best to help sick people." Then he got a phone call and said to me, "I'm sorry. I have a new patient. I have to go." He was very busy, but he looked lively.

I left the hospital. I thought about the two young men. "③What job is really good for me?" When I was walking to the station, an old woman suddenly fell down in front of me. She looked very sick and she couldn't talk. I thought she needed a doctor. I ran to the payphone and called an ambulance. After a while, the ambulance came.

Two hours later, her husband called me. He said, "She looked sick, but she is good now. It was kind of you to save my wife's life." He sounded very happy, and his words made me happy, too. I thought, "Life is the most important thing of all, and I am now interested in saving people's lives. There are a lot of jobs which can save lives, and a doctor is one of them. I want to be a doctor!" I told my sister about that. She was very glad to hear that.

　(注) trading company：貿易会社　　patient：患者　　lively：生き生きとした　　payphone：公衆電話
　　　ambulance：救急車

(1) 下線部①を日本語に直しなさい。

(2) 本文の内容に合うように（　ⓐ　），（　ⓑ　）にそれぞれ適当な日本語を入れなさい。

> 　（　ⓐ　）の職業に悩むスティーブに姉は，自分の（　ⓑ　）に会って，色々な職業の話を聞い
> たらどうか，というアイディアを出した。

(3) 下線部②の理由として最も適当なものを 1 つ選び，記号で答えなさい。

　ア　スティーブの相談を受けなければならなかったから。

　イ　救急車の運転を頼まれたから。

ウ　一晩中勤務をしていたから。

エ　新しい患者の予約が入っていたから。

(4)　下線部③のスティーブの気持ちとして最も適当なもの1つを選び，記号で答えなさい。

ア　つきたい職業が決まらず，とても迷っている気持ち

イ　つきたい職業が決まり，すがすがしい気持ち

ウ　職業について，もう話を聞きたくないという気持ち

エ　自分の得意な分野がわかり，安心した気持ち

(5)　本文の内容に一致するものを2つ選び，記号で答えなさい。

ア　Steve's sister said to him, "You must meet your friends more often."

イ　Steve was excited because his sister's friend in the trading company was working happily.

ウ　Steve couldn't listen to the doctor at all because he was too busy.

エ　The old woman told Steve to call the ambulance.

オ　The old woman's husband called Steve after going to the hospital.

カ　Steve decided to become a doctor because he already saved many lives.

総合問題 ③

1 右上の QR コードまたは CD の音声を聞き，次の問い（A，B）に答えなさい。

A それぞれの問いについて対話を聞き，答えとして最も適切なものを，ア〜エから選んで答えなさい。

(1) Why was Hans absent from school yesterday?　CD6 17

　　ア　He had a toothache.　　　　　　　イ　He was out of town.

　　ウ　He went to the dentist.　　　　　　エ　He caught a bad cold.　　　　（　　　）

(2) What will Kirara do on Sunday?　CD6 18

　　ア　She'll go to a concert.　　　　　　イ　She'll go to a flea market.

　　ウ　She'll call George.　　　　　　　エ　She'll meet George.　　　　（　　　）

B これから流れる英語を聞いて，それぞれの問いの答えとして最も適切なものをア〜エ
から選んで答えなさい。 CD6 19

(1) What is this announcement about?　　　　　　　　　　　　　　　　　（　　　）

出発 Departures			
ア	イ	ウ	エ

(2) What do students need to bring to the assembly?

　　ア　A box lunch.

　　イ　A notebook and a pen.

　　ウ　An exercise mat.

　　エ　A needle and a thread.　　　　　　　　　　　　　　　　　　　　（　　　）

(3) What will be handed out at the end of today's assembly?

　　ア　A list of the things you have to buy next Friday.

　　イ　A list of scholarships to be awarded by the universities.

　　ウ　A list of universities participating in the University Fair.

　　エ　A bus route map to the Civic Plaza from the school.　　　　　　（　　　）

2 次の各文の（　　）内に入る最も適当なものをそれぞれ1つ選び，記号で答えなさい。

(1) Which do you like (　　　), this or that?

　　ア　good　　　　　　イ　well　　　　　ウ　better　　　　エ　favorite

(2) My car is very old, but (　　　) looks new.

　　ア　you　　　　　　イ　your　　　　　ウ　yours　　　　エ　yourself

(3) Many lions (　　　) in this area.

ア　find　　　　　　イ　found　　　　　　ウ　are finding　　　エ　are found

(4) My father asked me (　　　) the car.

ア　wash　　　　　　イ　to wash　　　　　ウ　washed　　　　　エ　washing

(5) When I got home, my father (　　　) dinner in the kitchen.

ア　cooks　　　　　　イ　is cooked　　　　ウ　is cooking　　　エ　was cooking

(6) Look at that girl (　　　) is playing basketball.

ア　which　　　　　　イ　what　　　　　　ウ　whose　　　　　エ　who

(7) There is a picture (　　　) the wall.

ア　on　　　　　　　　イ　over　　　　　　ウ　beyond　　　　　エ　up

(8) I don't know (　　　) to do next.

ア　how　　　　　　　イ　that　　　　　　ウ　what　　　　　　エ　who

(9) We have not heard (　　　) our son in France since last year.

ア　without　　　　　イ　with　　　　　　ウ　to　　　　　　　エ　from

(10) "How (　　　) do you go to the movies?" "Well, once or twice a month."

ア　often　　　　　　イ　many　　　　　　ウ　much　　　　　　エ　fast

3 次の各日本文の意味を表すように，（　　　）内の語句を並べかえて正しい英文を作るとき，（　　　）内で 5 番目に来るものをそれぞれ 1 つ選び，記号で答えなさい。

(1) 母は牛乳を買いにスーパーマーケットに行ってきたところです。

My mother (buy / has / to / some milk / to / the supermarket / been).

ア　buy　　　　　　　イ　to　　　　　　　ウ　some milk　　　エ　the supermarket

(2) メアリーは何か部活動に所属していますか。

(Mary / to / activities / belong / does / any / club)?

ア　to　　　　　　　　イ　activities　　　　ウ　does　　　　　　エ　any

(3) これがその有名な芸術家によって描かれた絵です。

(the picture / by / artist / painted / this / the famous / is).

ア　the picture　　　　イ　by　　　　　　　ウ　artist　　　　　エ　painted

(4) 彼は怒って，さよならも言わずに部屋を出ていってしまった。

He (the room / got / saying / and / without / left / angry) goodbye.

ア　the room　　　　　イ　saying　　　　　ウ　without　　　　エ　angry

(5) 私の妹はまだ宿題を終えていません。

(her / my / finished / sister / little / homework / hasn't) yet.

ア　her　　　　　　　イ　finished　　　　ウ　sister　　　　　エ　homework

(6) あなたのクラスで最も速く走れるのは誰ですか。

(run / in / who / your / fastest / can / the) class?

ア　run　　　　　　　イ　your　　　　　　ウ　fastest　　　　エ　can

4 次の各日本文の意味を表すように，（　）内に適当な語を入れなさい。

(1) 去年の 8 月にたくさん雨が降りましたか。

Did you (　　　　　) (　　　　　　　　) rain last (　　　　　　)?

(2) お願いをしてもいいですか。

(　　　　　) I (　　　　　　) a favor (　　　　　) you?

(3) 私の姉はピアノが上手です。

My (　　　　　) is a (　　　　　) (　　　　　).

(4) 私は叔母ほど上手にお好み焼きをつくれません。

I (　　　　　) make Okonomiyaki (　　　　　) (　　　　　) (　　　　　) my aunt.

(5) 部屋を掃除するまで，母は私にテレビを見させてくれなかった。

My mother didn't (　　　　　) (　　　　　) (　　　　　) TV until I cleaned my room.

(6) 私は来月ホノルルを訪れるのを楽しみにしています。

I'm (　　　　　) (　　　　　) (　　　　　) (　　　　　) Honolulu next month.

(7) 私に何か温かい飲み物をください。

Please (　　　　　) (　　　　　) (　　　　　) (　　　　　) (　　　　　)
(　　　　　).

(8) あなたが私に貸してくれた雑誌は面白かった。

The magazine (　　　　　) (　　　　　) (　　　　　) (　　　　　) was interesting.

(9) デビンは丸い窓の家に住んでいます。

Devin lives in a house (　　　　　) (　　　　　) are round.

(10) カナリア諸島は多くの種類の鳥を見ることができる島々です。

The Canary Islands are the islands (　　　　　) (　　　　　) (　　　　　)
(　　　　　) many kinds of birds.

5 次の対話文は，ハワイに留学している日本人のタカ (Taka) が，友人のマイク (Mike) の家に電話をしたときのものです。これを読んで，あとの問いに答えなさい。

Mike's mother: Hello.

　　　　Taka: Hello. Is this Mike's mother?

Mike's mother: Yes. (　①　)

　　　　Taka: This is Taka speaking.

Mike's mother: Oh, Taka, aloha!

　　　　Taka: Aloha! (　②　)

Mike's mother: I'm sorry. He is out now, Taka. I think he will be back in an hour. (　③　)

　　　　Taka: No, thank you. I'll call back in an hour. Then, good-bye.

Mike's mother: OK. Good-bye.

----- An hour later -----

　　　　Mike: Hello.

Taka: Hello. Is this Mike?

Mike: Yes, speaking. I'm sorry I was out, surfing, when you called me.

Taka: No problem. Well, do you have a plan for next Sunday?

Mike: No, I don't. Why?

Taka: If you are free, I want to go shopping with you. February 24 is my mother's birthday. On that day, my family will have a party for her. I want to send her a present before the party. Can you go with me?

Mike: Yes, I can. I'd love to.

Taka: Mahalo! Thank you, Mike. Well, let's meet in front of the ABC bookstore at 10 o'clock.

Mike: OK. Let's enjoy shopping next Sunday. (　④　)

Taka: You're welcome. See you on Sunday.

(1)　(　①　)～(　④　)に入る最も適当なものをそれぞれ１つ選び，記号で答えなさい。

ア　Thank you for calling.　　　　イ　May I speak to Mike?

ウ　Wait a minute.　　　　　　　エ　Who's calling, please?

オ　Shall I take your message?　　カ　Why are you calling?

(2)　本文の内容に合うように(　ⓐ　)～(　ⓒ　)にそれぞれ適当な日本語を入れなさい。

> 　(　ⓐ　)月24日はタカのお母さんの誕生日である。そこで，今度の(　ⓑ　)曜日に友人のマイクと一緒にプレゼントを買いに行くことになった。二人はABC書店の(　ⓒ　)で10時に待ち合わせをすることになった。

6 次の文を読んで，あとの問いに答えなさい。

One day when Emily was a young girl, she went to the circus with her father. She was very much looking forward to seeing it. When they got there, there was a long line of people in front of the ticket office. Many of them were families with small children. Among them, the family in front of Emily and her father made a big impression on her. There were five children, all probably under the age of 12. They didn't seem to have much money. (　①　) The children stood nicely behind their mother and father. They were all excitedly talking about the lions, elephants and other acts they were going to see that night. ①It was not difficult to tell that it was their first time to see the circus.

The ticket lady said to the father, "How many tickets do you want?" He proudly said, "I'd like to buy five children's tickets and two adult tickets, please." The ticket lady said the price. The father put his head closer to the ticket lady and asked, "How much did you say?" The ticket lady repeated the price. (　②　)

Emily's father put his hand into his pocket, pulled out a $20 bill and dropped it on the ground. (　③　) "Excuse me, sir, this fell from your pocket."

②The man knew what was happening. He looked straight into her dad's eyes, took her dad's hand in both of his, and replied. "Thank you, thank you, sir. This is really important to me and my family."

Emily and her father went back to their car and drove home. ③They didn't go to the circus that night. But they were happy, anyway.

（注）circus：サーカス　　impression：印象　　probably：たぶん　　seem to ～：～のように思われる

　　　　act：出し物

(1)　（　①　）～（　③　）に入る最も適当なものをそれぞれ1つ選び，記号で答えなさい。

　　ア　He picked up the bill, and talked to the man.

　　イ　Their clothes were not expensive, but they were clean.

　　ウ　The man didn't have enough money for the tickets.

(2)　下線部①の内容として最も適切なもの1つ選び，記号で答えなさい。

　　ア　彼らは初めてサーカスを見に来たのだが，それは簡単なことだった。

　　イ　彼らは初めてサーカスを見たが，それはとても退屈だと感じた。

　　ウ　彼らがサーカスを見るのが初めてだということは，簡単に分かった。

　　エ　彼らがサーカスを見に来るのが困難だったということに初めて気づいた。

(3)　下線部②で，その男性は何がわかっていたのか。（　ⓐ　）～（　ⓒ　）にそれぞれ適当な日本語を入れなさい。

> エミリーの（　ⓐ　）が（　ⓑ　）をわざと落とし，男性が（　ⓒ　）ことにして渡してくれたこと。

(4)　下線部③で，サーカスを見ることができなかったのに'happy'であった理由として最も適切なものを1つ選び，記号で答えなさい。

　　ア　父親と娘で一緒に車で帰宅することができたから。

　　イ　男性とその家族がチケットを購入し，サーカスを見に行けたから。

　　ウ　男性が落とした財布を父親が拾ってあげて感謝されたから。

　　エ　チケット売り場で父親と男性が親しくなることができたから。

7　次の文を読んで，あとの問いに答えなさい。

Today I will tell you about a man I have known for about fifteen years. He was one of my students and his name is Kenji.

When he was seventeen years old, I asked him what he wanted to do in the future. He couldn't say anything.

One day he found a poster of a cookery school. It said, "We'll have an open house next Saturday. Let's enjoy cooking together!" He was interested in cooking and cooked for his family many times. So, he went there.

The students of the school welcomed him. He had a very good time there because he cooked with them and enjoyed the food. He thought, "Cooking is a lot of fun. If I become a cook, I can make many kinds of food. Good food can make people happy. I'll become a cook."

When he finished high school, he went to the cookery school. The classes were very difficult, but it was exciting for him to study something new every day. He studied very hard there to be a cook.

After he finished studying at the cookery school, he came to this city. He started to work for a Japanese restaurant. In his first year, he only washed the dishes. ①When he was washing the dishes, sometimes he watched the things that the other cooks did. This was his way of learning how to cook Japanese food.

One day in his second year, the master chef told him to cook lunch. Kenji was surprised. The master chef said, "I will watch how you cook. And if your lunch is good, you may help the other cooks." He watched how Kenji cooked.

He finished cooking, but ②the master chef didn't eat the lunch. Kenji asked him why. "You did your best today and I think you studied hard at the cookery school, but you didn't cook in my way... I know you feel sad, but I want all the cooks here to become good cooks. You must learn how to cook in my way first. After that, you can cook as you like. Don't rush. You have a lot of time."

Kenji faced many difficulties when he was working. Sometimes it was hard for him to overcome them, but he never gave up and became a good cook.

（注）cookery school：料理学校　　open house：体験入学

(1) 本文の内容に合うように（　ⓐ　）～（　ⓒ　）にそれぞれ適当な日本語を入れなさい。

> ケンジは高校生のとき先生に（　ⓐ　）をたずねられた際に，何も答えられなかった。ある日，彼は（　ⓑ　）の体験入学ポスターを見た。彼は（　ⓒ　）に興味があったので，それに参加してみた。

(2) 下線部①を日本語に直しなさい。

(3) 下線部②の理由として最も適当なものを１つ選び，記号で答えなさい。

　　ア　ケンジが最善を尽くしたのは見てわかったが，そのとき料理長は空腹でなかったから

　　イ　ケンジの料理学校での成績がよくなかったことをそっと耳打ちした者がいたから

　　ウ　ケンジの包丁さばきや調理手順が料理長のやり方と違っていたから

　　エ　ケンジが他の料理人仲間に味付けを手伝ってもらったことが判明したから

(4) ケンジの現在の年齢に最も近いものを１つ選び，記号で答えなさい。

　　ア　15歳　　　　　　　イ　17歳　　　　　　　ウ　32歳　　　　　　　エ　45歳

(5) 本文の話し手が，この話を通して伝えたかったこととして最も適切なものを１つ選び，記号で答えなさい。

　　ア　It is important to work hard for your dream.

　　イ　It is important to learn how to cook lunch.

　　ウ　It is important to study something new.

APPLAUSE
ENGLISH COMMUNICATION I
Workbook

編集　開隆堂編集部

発行　開隆堂出版株式会社

　　　代表者　岩塚太郎

　　　〒113-8608　東京都文京区向丘1-13-1

　　　電話03-5684-6115（編集）

　　　http://www.kairyudo.co.jp

印刷　株式会社大熊整美堂

販売　開隆館出版販売株式会社

　　　〒113-8608　東京都文京区向丘1-13-1

　　　電話03-5684-6118（販売）

■表紙デザイン

畑中 猛